Steve and Debbie Wilson

communication
the missing piece of the marriage puzzle

Published by Marriage Matters Now
Cross Roads, Texas, U.S.A.
www.MarriageMattersNow.com

ISBN 978-1-944244-45-3

Produced and packaged by Vision Book Producers. Stacie L. Jennings, Managing Editor; Jenny Avery, Line Editor; cover and interior design by Jeff Behymer/BeGraphic.

www.visionbookproducers.com

Table of Contents

Dedication

This book is dedicated to our children and grandchildren. Our prayer is that our legacy will continue to live through these precious people: Josh, Leigh, Morgan, Emmett, Jordan, Candace, Kenny, Janae, Hudson, and Harper.

Acknowledgement

We want to extend a very special thanks to Hershell and Cynthia Cavin, whose love and encouragement have meant more to us than words can adequately express. Thank you for believing so strongly in this project.

Foreword

One of the most challenging tasks we had as authors was to adequately demonstrate through our words the depth of emotion and passion that went into the creation of this book. The personal stories recounted herein were birthed from our blood, sweat, and tears—yet they reveal the true heart of our marriage.

When the two of us faced the hardest challenges of our marriage, we had no resources to help us navigate the treacherous path we were on. We walked blindly into dark areas of the soul that we never knew had to be exposed before our hearts could truly connect. We learned firsthand just how much work and perseverance it takes to attain—and retain—a strong emotional connection between a husband and wife.

We've written this book so that others might avoid some of the unnecessary heartache and struggle that oftentimes come against even the best of marriages. Our desire is that by sharing our experiences and what we've learned over the years, you'll be inspired to go to a deeper and more intimate level of communication with your spouse.

Every marriage has the potential to be a place of safety, one in which each spouse can experience the joy and peace that come from being both fully known—and fully loved. We invite you to walk with us through the six levels of communication that we identified on our own journey to wholeness. If you are willing to move to what you'll hear us refer to as "the deep end of the communication pool," you and your spouse can experience a love you never imagined possible. What's more, you'll have a more clear and vibrant understanding of God's love for you.

We pray that the small investment you make by sowing this book into your marriage will reap an ongoing harvest that continues for generations to come in your family.

Steve and Debbie Wilson

1

Blindsided

Blindsided. Sucker punched. Bushwhacked. No matter what name you give it, at some point we've each experienced an unexpected attack that sends us reeling: a colleague gets the promotion we thought we'd earned, the doctor delivers news that our biopsy came back positive, or our secretary tells us, "The IRS called. They need to schedule a meeting with you—today."

But who would ever anticipate being blindsided in the sanctity of your own home? Like when the kids are tucked safely in bed after coming home from the Wednesday night church service and you walk into the den carrying a big bowl of freshly popped popcorn, expecting to put your feet up and enjoy watching *The Tonight Show* with your wife. Instead, she looks you square in the eye and says, "Steve, if this is marriage, I don't think I want it anymore."

That's my story; it's *exactly* what happened to me. Apparently

1

Debbie—my beautiful wife of twelve years and the mother of our three children—had a drastically different perspective of our marriage than I did.

She never griped about anything major, so I always figured everything must be fine. Granted, we lived busy lives: I was the youth pastor at our church, and Debbie had a full-time job at home with the kids. At times we felt we were merely going through the motions of life, but wasn't that the norm for every couple with a young family?

We didn't have time to communicate much, which, in our case, was a good thing because it meant we didn't argue much. When we did argue, we'd both get defensive, so we'd come to an unspoken agreement: *We're in the ministry; everything will get better if we'll just suck it up and keep moving forward.*

Obviously, that strategy wasn't working as well as I thought because my wife had basically told me she wanted out.

If Debbie and I divorced, not only would I lose my wife and kids, but in our church denomination, I'd also lose my profession as a youth pastor.

Life as I knew it had come to an end.

You may say, "Well, Steve, why didn't the two of get some counseling?" You have to understand, this "blindside" incident happened a long time ago, when effective counseling was not available on a broad scope as it is today. At the time, there was literally nowhere Debbie and I could go to get the help we needed. And to be honest, if help *had* been available, I don't know if we'd have sought it out.

We were in the ministry; therefore, the fact that we were having problems meant something must be wrong with *us*. Neither of us would have allowed ourselves to be open and vulnerable in front of another person—especially someone at our own church.

Divorce was not an option for either of us, so Debbie and I came up with a plan of our own to save our marriage. Getting away together was the first critical step. We didn't have anyone to watch our children, who were then ages eleven, eight, and six, so we decided to spend a week on the beach in Gulf Shores, Alabama, where the kids could play—and we could talk.

Although Debbie's declaration "If this is marriage, I don't think I want it anymore" marked the worst day of my life, it also marked the beginning of the best days. The next morning I went to my pastor and said, "I have to go out of town. Debbie and I are leaving tomorrow with the kids, and I'll be back in a week."

He looked at me warily over his reading glasses and asked, "Is everything okay?"

Without hesitation I smiled and said yes. (After all, I was on staff at a church, which meant I had to have it all together—all of the time.)

When I was a senior in high school, our church regularly hosted a singing group from a college in Missouri. This group of Christian students frequently performed at churches in our area. Our family got to know several of the members pretty well, including one young man, a junior named Steve Wilson. Mom and Dad developed a special relationship with Steve, and the three of them stayed in touch even after I graduated from high school and went on to attend Baylor University.

When I was in high school, I dated a young man for a couple of years; I truly thought he was the one I would marry. However, in my senior year I realized he did not want the same things in life that I did. So I broke off the relationship and went to Baylor, where I was sure God had the right man for me. I knew God had something significant for me, so I was determined to wait upon Him and believe for His best in my life.

In January of my senior year at Baylor, Steve, who was now a youth pastor outside the Kansas City area, called my parents to ask about our family. When he asked about me, my mother gave him my phone number, and he immediately called me.

We talked. And talked. And talked some more.

With the Lord as our common bond, over the next few weeks we developed a long-distance relationship built upon hours of open and honest conversation. We shared our hearts, our souls, and our love of the Lord.

During one of our conversations, Steve asked if I would come to Kansas City and hang out with him over an upcoming school break. (I would be staying in his pastor's home.) I said yes. My friends teased that I was going to come back engaged; I told them they were all crazy.

Although I was old enough that I didn't need my parents' permission to make such a decision, I still valued their input. So the following weekend I went home to Houston and told them about my plans. Dad asked some questions, and then surprised me when he said he and Mom would come pick me up at the end of the visit. When I told

Steve about their decision to come to Kansas City, he expressed his delight at the idea of seeing them again.

When I got to Kansas City, I was delighted when Steve told me he had tickets for an Evie Tournquist concert. On the way to the concert, something happened that let me know Steve was the man for me. We were driving down the highway, talking, when all of a sudden Steve slowed down. When I asked what he was doing, he said, "We just passed a woman on the side of the road with a flat tire. I'm going back to help her."

I was blown away by his care and compassion for someone he didn't know; I'd never witnessed anything like it before. I knew at that moment he was the godly man I was waiting for, and I couldn't wait to see how the rest of the evening played out. We had a great time at the concert, where we saw many people who held places of significance in Steve's life. I met many of his friends that night.

On the drive home after the concert, Steve asked if I would like to go to the church where he was serving and pray together before we called it a night. I said yes. We had prayed together over the phone for the past three months, so praying together in person for the first time did not seem unusual.

When we got to the church, we went into the sanctuary, sat down on the first pew, and began to talk. Steve said, "I'm having some strange feelings, Debbie. I know we haven't really dated, but as we sit here in this church, I feel the Lord telling me we're supposed to marry."

How do you respond to something like that? As shocking as Steve's statement was, in my heart I was feeling the same thing—and I told him so.

We prayed that night—believe me, we prayed—and asked God to give us a physical sign to confirm what we were sensing was His will, not ours. After we asked God for that confirming sign, we walked out of the church trusting He would show us. And then we kissed for the first time.

The next morning I called my parents, and Mom answered the phone. Before I had a chance to say anything, she asked me a question, which by the tone of her voice was clearly not a casual one: "Deb, what's going on?"

"Mom, I can't explain it, but Steve and I feel like we're supposed to get married."

For what seemed like an eternal three seconds, she was silent. When at last she spoke, her words stunned me. "We knew when we met Steve four years ago he was the man for you."

Mom and I talked for a few more minutes, and then she put Dad on the phone so that I could tell him.

"So ... what do you think, Dad?" I asked.

In a strong voice he said, "If God is for you, who can be against you?"

When my parents arrived at the end of the weekend, Steve met with my father and asked for my hand. As my girlfriends had predicted, I returned to Baylor with a ring on my finger.

Steve was already in full-time ministry, and because I'd been saved since the age of seven, I thought, *Wow! This is going to be the most amazing Christian marriage.* The way I saw it, if we loved each other and we loved Jesus, then surely we had the exact formula for success.

So Steve and I were married. And then we jumped right into ministry together.

Notice I didn't say we jumped into marriage; we jumped into ministry.

Steve and I knew how to do ministry; unfortunately, we didn't know how to do marriage. Thirty-seven years ago we didn't have access to premarital counseling (at least the kind that was actually beneficial to two people about to take the biggest step of their lives). Counseling wouldn't have changed my decision to marry Steve; however, it would have been helpful if someone had told me that entering marriage would be the most challenging thing I'd ever do. No one told me that, so there I was living in la-la land, thinking everything would automatically be great all of the time.

And it was for a while.

But somewhere around the seventh year of marriage, I began to feel like I was losing Steve. Was I losing him physically? No. Was he trying to get away from me and from making an investment in our marriage? No. Nothing was going on that I could pinpoint, yet I felt myself disconnecting from him. I thought about talking to him about how I felt, but experience had taught me that addressing issues in our marriage only put both of us on defense, and we usually ended up blaming each other. Besides, I didn't know what to say to him. So I let it go, telling myself, "It's going to get better, Debbie. It's going to get better."

By the time we'd been married twelve years, it wasn't better. In fact, the distance between us was growing.

That Wednesday night was no different from any other.

I saw to it that the kids got to their classes, and I attended the midweek youth service with Steve. Our three children were still young, so the goal after church was always to get them home, give them a snack, and get them bathed and into bed quickly because they were grouchy—and so were we. Once the kids were in bed, Steve would go to the kitchen and prepare a big bowl of popcorn, which is what he did that night.

I honestly hadn't given any thought to what was about to come out of my mouth, but as my husband picked up the remote to turn on *The Tonight Show*, I said, "Steve, don't turn that on." He had no clue what was about to take place (other than maybe thinking something nice was happening).

Then I said the words no husband ever wants to hear: "We've gotta talk."

I had no idea what to say next, but I'd gone this far and wasn't going to turn back. He stood there looking at me like a deer in the headlights as I blurted out, "Steve, if this is marriage, I don't think I want it anymore."

Did I consciously want a divorce? No—all I knew was something had to change. Since realizing five years earlier that we were disconnecting, I'd become emotionally numb. I didn't *want* to feel any emotions—especially when it seemed the only emotion we expressed in our home was anger. I was at the point where I felt so alone that I reasoned it would be better to be lonely by myself than to be lonely with him.

One thing I've learned from my own experience is this: The loneliest women in the world are not single women; the loneliest women in the world are married women. (The same can be true for men, as well.) The reason people are lonely in marriage is that, as couples, we do not know how to connect to each other. We don't know how to communicate. We don't know what to do when it comes to being married.

Because of this naïve belief, we struggled in our marriage for twelve long years—until the night I dropped the bomb: "If this is marriage, I don't think I want it anymore."

Did we separate? No.

Did we leave each other? No.

We had no one to turn to with our problem, no books to read and no conferences to attend. But we had God, and when we turned to Him, He helped us figure out how to fix our marriage. Now we have not only a good marriage—we have a great marriage!

Steve

As married men, we often wonder, if we have kids, a house, a dog, two cars—and sex every once in a while—what else do our wives need from us?

Well, in my case there was an essential emotional connection that was missing in Debbie's and my relationship.

When we packed our car and left that Thursday morning for the beach, Debbie and I had no idea what our problem was— let alone how to solve it. The only thing we knew was divorce was not an option. We were depending on God to intervene and do something with our seemingly impossible situation.

For the next six days, while the kids built sandcastles and romped in the waves, Debbie and I sat together in beach chairs and regurgitated our frustrations with our relationship. Through that initial clearing of the air, God revealed that over the past twelve years we'd actually neglected our own hearts. We'd lost the ability to look at each other with genuine care and ask, "How is your heart?" Because we had originally established our relationship with hours of verbal communication, we assumed this pattern would continue after we were married. But then life happened.

Although Debbie and I made significant progress that week at the beach, the day before we were to go home, I found Debbie sitting in her beach chair, crying. When I asked what was wrong, she said, "I'm afraid we'll go home and nothing will change."

That's when we came up with our plan.

We decided that, no matter how busy we were, we would take time to sit down together every single day for ten to fifteen minutes and ask each other, "How is your heart?" Then we would listen—truly listen—to what we each had to say. We made a vow to be loving with our questions and honest with our answers. The health of our hearts and the life of our marriage depended on it.

As we were praying together the night before we left the beach house, the Lord reminded us of the words Debbie's father had spoken thirteen years earlier: "If God is for you, who can be against you?" Then the Lord impressed us to turn to Philippians 1:6, where we found this assuring promise: "[Be] confident of this very thing, that He who has begun a good work in you will complete it until the day of Jesus Christ."

Our circumstances didn't change overnight. It took us twelve years to get into our mess, and it took some time to get out of it. But the work God began in our hearts that week at the beach has borne much fruit. Today Debbie and I travel up to thirty weekends each year conducting marriage conferences, while the Lord works through us to bring about the most amazing restorations in people's lives and marriages.

We learned through our own experience that marriage is hard work. We went into marriage thinking if we had each other and we had Jesus, we had all we needed. After all, the Bible says, "Two are better than one, because they have a good reward for their labor. For if they fall, one will lift up his companion. Though one may be overpowered by another, two can withstand him. And a threefold cord is not quickly broken" (Ecclesiastes 4:9–10, 12). These verses paint a beautiful picture of a threefold covenant marriage between a man, a woman, and God. Notice, the Bible doesn't say that a threefold cord *cannot* be broken but, rather, that it cannot be *quickly* broken.

Debbie and I now know the reason our marriage began to unravel was that a piece of our foundation was missing. That piece was *communication*. At the time we were struggling, there were no resources we could lay hold of. No books, no CDs or DVDs, no conferences. The book you now hold in your hand contains the insights and biblical truths God revealed to us over the years. It was those truths that saved our marriage.

Debbie and I wrote this book because we have an undeniable passion to get right in the middle of where people live and help them get to the place they want to be.

You may have purchased this book yourself, or perhaps your spouse gave it to you. Maybe you're reading it because you want to make a good marriage better; however, you may be reading it and thinking, *If something drastic doesn't happen soon, I'm headed for divorce.* If this is you, let me assure you, you're not alone. Debbie and I can be with you on the pages of this book, and God is with you right where you are, right now. Best of all, He has a plan for you, as His Word promises: "'For I know the thoughts that I think toward you,' says the LORD, 'thoughts of peace and not evil, to give you a future and a hope'" (Jeremiah 29:11).

Whether your marriage needs no more than a little tweaking to make it a great marriage or it needs a complete overhaul, I want to invite you to join Debbie and me on a redemptive journey of faith. We will share our own experiences and struggles, and reveal how God's love and faithfulness brought healing to our broken hearts and restoration to our marriage.

You'll probably laugh a little, and perhaps you'll cry. But if you're willing to take an honest look at your own heart and see your spouse and marriage through God's eyes, you'll be able to tap into the future and the hope that's already yours.

After all, as a wise man once said, *"If God is for you, who can be against you?"*

2

Wading in the Baby Pool

> So then, my beloved brethren, let every man be
> swift to hear, slow to speak, slow to wrath.
> James 1:19

Debbie and I returned from our week at the beach committed to sit down every day and ask each other, "How is your heart?" Other than doing that, we had no idea how God was going to repair our fractured relationship. We put our trust in God and our faith in His Word; He would reveal each subsequent step as we were required to take it. I guess that's why the Bible says God's Word is "a lamp to my feet and a light to my path" and not a spotlight on the future (see Psalms 119:105).

One of the first steps we took together came in the form of a trip to the furniture store—I'm not kidding—where we purchased a chair. Not just any chair. This chair was dark green and had huge cushions and arms. Though it wasn't quite big enough to have its own zip code, it had plenty of space for two people to sit comfortably together, yet it was intimate enough to provide a sense of safety. It was in this chair that Debbie and

I began our journey to wholeness and subsequently gained an understanding of how vital communication is in the life of a marriage.

We learned that we each needed to be swift to hear, slow to speak, and slow to anger if we wanted to communicate effectively and thus change the course of our marriage. As we prayed together and followed the leading of the Lord, we identified six specific levels of communication that we experienced on our journey to wholeness:

- Making small talk
- Sharing facts
- Expressing opinions
- Expressing feelings
- Expressing needs
- Sharing beliefs

Most of us are experts at the first two levels, making small talk and sharing facts. While small talk and sharing facts are an essential part of daily life, a marriage cannot survive at this level. The sad thing is, the majority of married couples—both Christian and non-Christian—never make it past the first two levels. Like Debbie and I, they never get to the place of deep emotional connection that cements their relationship. It's like wading in the baby pool when they could be enjoying a real swim in the grown-up pool.

To further complicate matters, men and women don't always communicate on the same wavelength. The following story about a couple named Wade and Donna illustrates this point.

After more than twenty years of marriage, Wade decided he wanted to do something special for his wife's upcoming birthday. The more he deliberated about what to do, the more nervous and fearful he became at the thought of not getting it right. Instead of trying to plan a surprise, he decided to ask Donna what she wanted for her birthday.

One evening as Donna was preparing dinner, Wade walked into the kitchen and said, "Hey, honey, do you know you've got a birthday coming up in a couple of weeks?"

"Yeah, yeah, yeah ... so what?"

"Well, what would you like for your birthday?"

Without taking her eyes off of the stove, she said, "I don't care."

"Oh no, I want you to tell me what you want."

Now remember, she was right in the middle of cooking dinner. Not the best time for a conversation about her birthday.

But Wade persisted. "I'm not leaving the kitchen until you tell me."

"Okay, Wade. If you want to know what I really want, it's to be six again!"

He thought, *Perfect. I can work with this.* So for the next two weeks, he planned her birthday down to the smallest detail. When the big morning arrived, he said, "Happy birthday, honey! I want you to get up and get dressed—wear something casual. I have the whole day planned for you."

Donna rolled her eyes and said okay, all the while thinking, *This should be interesting.*

They got in the car and drove to the local amusement park, where for the next three hours they rode every ride, ate cotton candy, and played games. When Wade said, "Okay, we're leaving," Donna thought, *Great, because I can't do this anymore.* They got back in the car, but they didn't go home. Instead, Wade drove to the movie theater where he purchased popcorn, candy, and a giant soft drink to enjoy as they watched the latest animated kids' movie.

When they left the theater, Donna said, "Okay, Wade, this

was great, but now please take me home."

Wade couldn't hide his excitement. "Just one more stop," he said. He pulled the car up in front of McDonald's, ceremoniously escorted her inside, and then bought her a Happy Meal and made her play on the playground.

When they got home an hour later, Donna collapsed on the sofa. Her stomach hurt, her head hurt, even her toenails hurt. But Wade didn't have a clue that she was miserable; he was so proud of himself, he was about to burst.

"So, honey, you said you wanted to be six again for your birthday. What was it like?"

Donna looked at her husband as only a wife can do and said, "Wade, I meant my dress size. I want to be *size* six!"

Okay, so Wade and Donna are characters of my imagination. But the point I want to make is this: oftentimes our wives don't tell us what they're really thinking, and just as often we husbands may not be truly listening.

That's why it's imperative that we don't camp out forever in the baby pool of communication.

Level One: Making Small Talk

In the baby pool of communication, small talk reigns supreme. Everybody knows how to do small talk; it's what we do with high school friends or college roommates. Remember what that was like? You're coming and going, talking about the easy stuff, nothing really deep.

Small talk equates to about twelve inches of water in the baby pool. You think you're swimming, but you're not. Small talk is not threatening, it's not risky, and it's not going to get you in trouble. You're certainly not going to drown. Making small talk is what you do with people in the grocery store or at church. Small talk has no depth.

Making small talk comes naturally to most women. Nobody taught me how to make small talk, and Steve and I certainly didn't teach our daughter, Janae, how to make small talk. When she was a child and we'd lay her down for a nap, she would talk to herself for the longest time. Then suddenly she'd drop off to sleep. Sometimes she would wake up and finish the sentence she'd been saying as she'd fallen to sleep, and we'd ask, "How did she do that?" Our boys, Josh and Jordan, were never like that; all they did was grunt. (If you've raised boys, you know exactly what I'm talking about.)

The top three reasons people cite when divorcing are financial struggles, sexual issues, and the inability to communicate effectively. Although we can't deny the causes of divorce, we can take a good look at what to do to counteract these hurdles, especially when it comes to communication. Steve and I have learned the reason people stay stuck in the small-talk level of communication is due to one or more of the following three factors.

First is *busyness.* We live in a culture that never slows down. As married couples, we are involved in numerous activities. We follow suit by placing our children in multiple activities including sports, arts, and church or school functions. We don't give ourselves time to simply chill and enjoy one another, and then we wonder why our families are falling apart. We need more time together as couples and families to play, laugh, and talk about life.

Second is *technology*. Whether we want to admit it or not, we are addicted to technology. It is rare for couples and families to sit and talk to one another without looking at some kind of device, such as a phone, computer, or the TV. We are raising a generation of children who feel they have to be constantly entertained. The net result of this dependency on technology is that we are not *present* when we are with each other. Much of our self-worth and value to others is found in eye contact and undivided attention. Our families are losing their sense of worth because we are competing with electronic devices. Remember, you are in control of balancing what is best for your marriage and family.

The third factor that limits our communication to small talk is *apathy*. Sad to say, but couples quit working at communication way too quickly. We've bought into the idea that life should be easy, so when we give up on communication, we miss the benefits of wisdom and growth. Real love demands sacrifice and perseverance.

Most communication in our homes is small talk. Small talk isn't necessarily a bad thing, especially when we're in the middle of a busy day. However, if we want our relationships to deepen, we have to be intentional about moving past the small talk. We have to choose to move out of our comfort zone. We need to change our attitude and decide that to have the best marriage and family relationships, we must choose to work—and work hard—at communicating.

Level Two: Sharing Facts

The other baby-pool level of communication we must move past is sharing facts.

We exchange facts every day. "I picked up the clothes at the cleaners." "The school program starts at seven-thirty." "Your mom called today; she wants to talk to you about your dad's birthday." We exchange facts on a daily basis; doing so is a necessity. However, sharing facts does not solidify a marital relationship.

For the first twelve years of our marriage, Steve and I remained in the baby pool of communication, engaging in small talk and sharing facts, never moving to a deeper level of communication that would strengthen and develop our relationship. No wonder I felt as if I were losing him; we were disconnecting. When it came to communicating, we were doing only what was easy, the bare minimum.

We returned home from our week at the beach determined to spend time daily deepening our communication level. Let me tell you, doing so was uncomfortable; it didn't feel natural. When Steve asked, "How's your heart?" my baby-pool response would have been "fine." But I'd made the decision I wasn't going to answer that way anymore because I never wanted to lose him again.

For us, the question had taken on a deeper meaning than before. Today when Steve asks about my heart, here's what I hear: "Tell me what's going on in your heart. Tell me if I've done anything to hurt your heart today, because now I want to fix it. Share with me how you're feeling."

I believe most marriages are like ours was. One spouse

will have a greater desire than the other spouse to deepen his or her level of communication. Steve and I had to take the time and make the effort to move forward. We had to build up ourselves, and we had to build up our faith as the Bible directs: "But you, beloved, build yourselves up on [the foundation of] your most holy faith [continually progress, rise like an edifice higher and higher]" (Jude 1:20 AMP).

Perhaps you are the spouse least motivated to move forward, as I was. If so, hang in there with us. By the time you finish this book, you'll understand the multifaceted rewards of moving out of the entrapment of the communication baby pool.

———◆———

Steve

Debbie said moving to a deeper level of communication was uncomfortable. Can I just tell you, that may be the biggest understatement in this book?

Sure, I desired to connect with Debbie's heart so that I could understand what made her tick. But I didn't know what that kind of connecting looked like. I discovered I first needed to take a hard look at myself—and then change my behavior. For example, I realized it was easy for me to listen to her tell me about a good day, but when she wanted to share a bad day, I would roll my eyes and think, *Okay, here we go again.* So I began choosing to say instead, "Okay, tell me about it." Then I would *listen with my heart* as she told me about her day.

Simply put, I had to change my perspective about our relationship. I did this by picturing myself alone on an island with Debbie and saying, "You know what? We're in this together. I've got you and you've got me. Life's going to be okay." With that perspective, it was easy to discover what made the flame in her heart flicker. (And I made sure to put plenty of fuel on it to make it burn hotter each day.)

Debbie and I have done a lot of counseling in recent years, and it's been mind-boggling to see how many people divorce who had been married more than twenty-five years. In some instances, the kids were grown and gone, and the couple held the false notion the grass was greener somewhere else. We've seen other couples who apparently had their fingers crossed when they went to the altar, because they already had an exit strategy in place. When life got tough, these couples had no commitment to stand on.

Can I get sideways with you for a minute? The grass is *not* greener on the other side—it's AstroTurf! It's fake. Someone enters into an affair and thinks, *Wow—this is awesome!* It's not. It's like a trip to Disney World. Lots of people visit, but who lives there? Mickey Mouse. Once the park closes each evening, people go home to reality. They feed their kids and their dogs, and then they scoop the poop in the yard.

Having an affair is not reality. Reality is life at home. You and your spouse may have a hard time communicating; you may not like each other at times. The troubles are real, but so is the love—and that's what's authentic.

There are a multitude of reasons a couple may choose to divorce, but let's take a minute to review the top three. Number one is *financial struggles*, number two is problems with *sex*, and number three is *ineffective communication*. Do you think if couples could learn how to communicate effectively, they might be able to figure out how to deal with finances and sex? Debbie and I believe this is true.

If we want to be successful in dealing with the weightier issues of marriage, we've got to quit wading in the baby pool of communication. We have to learn to go deeper. But before we move into the deeper waters of the third level of communication, Debbie and I want give you a life jacket in the form of four things to do that will ensure your head remains above water.

3

The Four Safety-Building Be's

> *You're here to be salt-seasoning that brings out the*
> *God-flavors of this earth. If you lose your saltiness,*
> *how will people taste godliness?*
> Matthew 5:13 *THE MESSAGE*

Many have described the Sermon on the Mount as the great manifesto of the kingdom of God. In this discourse found in Matthew 5–7, Jesus gave guidelines for dealing with our relationships with both God and others. In essence, Jesus was building a place of safety for believers as they charted the deep waters of life. These guidelines are commonly known as "the beatitudes."

As Debbie and I charted the ever-deepening waters of communication, we discovered our own version of the beatitudes, which we now refer to as "the four safety-building be's." Each of these "be's" was a vital component in deepening our communication:

- Be honest
- Be understanding

- Be connected
- Be willing

You may say, "But, Steve, you don't understand what a mess my marriage is in. There's no way my spouse and I could be honest, understanding, connected, and willing. It's not the way we are."

This may be true. But each of these character traits begins with a choice. When you make the *choice* to be honest, understanding, connected, and willing, God will help you. All you have to do is ask. The Bible says, "Let us therefore come boldly to the throne of grace, that we may obtain mercy and find grace to help in time of need" (Hebrews 4:16). One you've connected with God's grace, you can make the same confident declaration that the apostle Paul made: "I can do all things through Christ who strengthens me" (Philippians 4:13).

So now, let's take a look at each of these four be's so that we can build an environment that allows us to move toward the deep end of the communication pool.

Be Honest

When Steve and I first made the choice to be honest with each other, we realized that doing so could be either a good or a bad thing. Neither of us wanted to use honesty as an attack tool, so we inserted an addendum: be honest *with honor*. The biblical definition of the word *honor* is "value, dignity, esteem of the highest degree." Now let me tell you why honesty with honor was one of the initial components that God revealed to us.

For years, Steve knew something wasn't right with me. He would ask, "Are you okay?" And you know what I would say? The same thing most of us women say, "Yeah, I'm fine."

If we're going to move forward in our marriages, we have to decide to open our mouths and speak—with honesty and honor.

I can only wonder how our lives might have been different if, eight years into our marriage, I'd said, "Steve, I feel as if you don't pursue me anymore—and I miss it," or "I'm hurt when I see the time, compassion, and mercy you give others at church. But when we get home, the kids and I get only what's left of you." Instead of being honest, I engaged in a game of cat and mouse to get him to find out what was bothering me.

I didn't realize that when I said I was fine, I was actually making it hard for Steve to come close to me. Here's a news flash: If you're going to act like a porcupine, your spouse isn't going to want to come near you! He's not going to pursue you, saying, "Please, please, *please*, tell me what's wrong." It's not going to happen.

Your spouse cannot read your mind. Steve once said to me, "Debbie, you're going to *have* to tell me what's bothering you." I replied, "Well, it's not going to mean the same if I have to tell you." I played these games with Steve on a regular basis, but the sad thing was, neither of us ever won.

You may think once Steve and I made the decision

to walk in honesty with honor in our communication, everything was fine. It wasn't. We had to *learn* how to communicate with each other. Remember, at that time no resources existed for us to turn to; we had to figure out the whole communication thing for ourselves through trial and error. For instance, here's a common communication error that I'm sure plays out in many marriages:

He says, "Honey, can we talk about finances?"

She says, "Sure."

He says, "You know, last month we spent more than we took in."

She says, "There you go again! You're always bringing that up and accusing me!"

Sound familiar? Regardless of the issue—finances, children, sex, or whatever—if our spouses don't feel *safe enough* to talk to us, they're not going to. When we say, "There you go, bringing that up again," they're going to walk away, vowing never to "go there" again. Each time this happens, the wall between us will grow a little higher.

One thing I had to learn about being honest with honor was how to approach my husband. Rather than bluntly telling him about something that was bothering me, which he might easily have heard as my being critical or condemning of him, I prefaced my comments with, "Steve, I need you to hear my heart about something. I'm not finding fault with you; I only want you to know what's going on with me."

Learning to honor your spouse while being honest with him or her will open up your communication in ways you never dreamed possible. Perhaps that's why the Bible says, "Let love be without hypocrisy. Abhor what is evil. Cling to what is good. Be kindly affectionate to one another with brotherly love, *in honor* giving preference to one another" (Romans 12:9–10, italics added).

Be Understanding

I think being understanding is one of the most effective tools in making a marriage better. To accomplish this, every once in a while, we need to take a walk in our spouse's shoes.

I know for Steve and me, when things are going well, it's easy to make life about God. But when things aren't going so well, life becomes "all about me." When it comes to the topic of understanding, many of us only consider ourselves. We want to be heard; therefore, we feel the need to defend ourselves.

If we truly want to move to a deeper level of communication with our husband or wife, we have to put ourselves in our spouse's shoes. Case in point: I was a stay-at-home mom, raising three children. When Steve walked in the door from work, guess what? I was ready for some adult conversation. But what was Steve *not* ready to do? You guessed it—talk.

As a counselor at our church, Steve talked all day long, more than most men like to talk. I had to consider this fact and then do what Romans 12:10 instructs me to do: give "preference to" him.

It wasn't until Steve began counseling on a full-time basis and invited me to help him that I truly understood what it was like to walk in his shoes. Now, when we finish counseling for the day, we go home and sit on the porch together. We are so grateful for each other. Apart from

31

saying, "I love you," we often sit in quietness because we have made the choice to understand one another.

In choosing to walk in each other's shoes, Steve and I opened our communication to an infusion of compassion, understanding, and sympathy we had never before experienced. Today, as we counsel young couples about this issue, we like to point out to the wife that her husband may go every day to a job he doesn't even like so that he can take care of their family. We also remind the husband that while he's at work talking to adults all day, his wife may not have a single opportunity to talk to another adult. She may talk only to their children as she cares for them and doles out discipline.

Bottom line, there are many dynamics in a marriage that require understanding on both the husband's and the wife's part.

---◆---

Steve

Men aren't the only ones who may be working at a job they don't like. Many women are doing the same thing—in addition to raising children. I can tell you from years of experience in counseling, women often beat themselves up over having to put their kids in childcare. So when your wife comes home from work and you think she is being moody, instead of asking, "What's wrong with you?" how about asking, "Okay, honey, what's going on with you today?"

I'm not taking sides; rather, I'm pointing out how important it is for married couples to understand what's going on with each other. Being understanding has a direct impact in the emotional climate of the home.

For instance, when our kids were young and Debbie was home with them, she and I made an agreement. When I got home, I would rest a little bit before engaging with the family. This brief respite made a world of difference in the way I communicated with Debbie and the way she responded to me when I'd say, "Debbie, tell me what I can do that would help you the most this evening."

I remember one evening she said, "After dinner, if you would bathe the kids, I'd really appreciate it." Being a sanguine personality, I decided the kids and I were going to have a party. And that's exactly what we did; we had ourselves some bath-time fun!

When Debbie came into the bathroom, she said, "Just look at the floor, Steve—there's water everywhere!"

She was right, of course, but I told her, "If you want me to bathe the kids, this is how I'm going to do it. We might be throwing towels at each other, and we might get water all over the place. But, Debbie, rejoice in this: When it's all over, I'm going to get a towel and clean the floor. And when I'm done, you'll have a clean bathroom."

She actually liked that perspective. While I was bathing the kids, she had time to slow down and switch from "mommy mode" to "wife mode." I can tell you from personal experience, there are times when being understanding reaps its own special benefits.

Be Connected

Okay, so we've talked about being honest with honor and

being understanding, both of which are important. But being connected is critical.

There came a time when Debbie and I realized we'd become disconnected, and I'm not talking about sex. I can almost hear some men saying, "How else are you going to connect?" What we have to understand is, for men, sex is a physical act. For women, it's an emotional act. If I want to be with Debbie once the kids are bathed and in bed, I must first connect to her emotionally. I need to connect to her heart; I need to understand what's going on with her.

When Debbie and I first started talking openly and honestly with each other about being connected, it surprised me to learn the thing that made her feel most connected with me was not sex. She felt most connected when we were playing and having fun together.

Clearly, we had not been on the same page throughout the first decade of our marriage.

Debbie and I are both competitive. Now that we no longer have children at home, we often have dinner together and then get out the cards for a fierce game of crazy eights. She'll taunt me, saying, "I'm going to beat you!" I'll say, "No, I'm going to beat *you*!" We'll laugh until we're in tears, but when it's ready to turn out the lights for the evening, we're emotionally connected and comfortable with whatever happens next.

It's unfortunate that once we become adults, we often quit having fun. Who said being a grown-up means putting all fun behind us? Certainly, we should put all irresponsibility behind us, as the Bible says: "When I was a child, I spoke as a child, I understood as a child, I thought as a child; but when I became a man, I put away childish things" (1 Corinthians 13:11).

Nothing will connect you more than laughing and having

fun together. And once you've connected emotionally, the physical connection is a natural outcome!

Be Willing to Communicate

Jesus once said, "The spirit is indeed willing, but the flesh is weak" (Matthew 26:41). He said this in the context of His disciples falling asleep while praying, but the principle is the same. In the natural, we may not know *how* to communicate at a deeper level. All the Lord is asking of us is to *be willing*.

God has already given us His Holy Spirit, whom Jesus referred to as the Spirit of truth, saying, "He will guide you into all truth" (John 16:13). The apostle Paul said, "Likewise the Spirit also helps us in our weaknesses" (Romans 8:26). The Holy Spirit is a trustworthy teacher, counselor, and guide who will lead you step-by-step to a deeper level of communication with your spouse.

As I said at the beginning of this chapter, each one of these four be's, or character traits, begins with a choice. We must *choose* to be honest, understanding, connected, and willing to communicate with our spouses at a deeper level.

Was putting these traits into practice always easy for Debbie and me? No.

Did we make mistakes? Yes.

Was moving to a deeper level of communication worth the effort? Yes, yes ... *yes!*

And I can tell you from personal experience, once you make the choice to follow God's plan for your marriage, you'll find that His grace is more than sufficient to meet your every need.

4

Whitewater Rafting to the Deep End

> *They speak from the [viewpoint of the] world*
> *[with its immoral freedom and baseless theories—*
> *demanding compliance with their opinions and*
> *ridiculing the values of the upright.*
> 1 John 4:5 AMP

Between the calm waters of the baby pool and the deep waters of the adult pool lies level three of communication: expressing opinions. It's a treacherous area that I refer to as "the whitewater rapids" of communication.

Understanding this level is crucial. We'll never move to the deep end of the communication pool if we don't master this level, which is why we're going to spend some time here.

Debbie and I found that, in most marriages, one spouse is more strongly opinionated than the other. When we are conducting a live conference, at this point I always tell the audience, "This is not the time to raise your hand or elbow your spouse."

Having a strong opinion is not necessarily a bad thing. It's actually a leadership characteristic, or gift, that was given to us by God for the purpose of being a blessing to others as we fulfill His unique call on our lives. However, when we don't understand that this gift, like all gifts from God, operates by love, we get into trouble.

Here's what the Bible says: "And He Himself gave some to be apostles, some prophets, some evangelists, and some pastors and teachers, for the equipping of the saints for the work of the ministry, for the edifying of the body of Christ ... that we should no longer be children, tossed to and fro and carried about with every wind of doctrine ... but, *speaking the truth in love*, may grow up in all things into Him who is the head—Christ—from whom the whole body, joined and knit together by what every joint supplies ... causes growth of the body for the edifying of itself *in love*" (Ephesians 4:11–16, italics added).

Regardless of our individual personalities and unique gifts, the Bible instructs us to speak the truth *in love* so that we edify others. Communicating *in love* is God's way. It's the way He intended relationships to work. Sadly, many spouses have not yet learned how to walk in love. They refuse to relinquish their strong opinions. Instead, they assume this position in their marriages: "Honey, feel free to have an opinion. But when you're ready to form the right opinion—I'm here for you."

I can just hear Dr. Phil asking, "How's that working for you?" The funny thing is, this position actually *does* work for the highly opinionated person. When the spouse rolls his or her eyes, says okay, and then walks away, the opinionated person thinks, *Well, I must be right.*

Strongly opinionated people who think they are right all the time do not value their spouses. The spouses may put up with this behavior over an extended period of time, but at some point the guillotine is going to come down. They will say, "You know what, I'm not going to put up with this anymore. I'm done."

And then a cycle begins. The opinionated spouse will say, "I'm sorry," and things will be okay for a while. But without intervention, sooner or later both spouses will revert to the familiar behavior that only builds a wall of separation between them.

When I was still on staff at the church, I remember counseling one such couple I'll refer to as Bob and Molly. Prior to their first session, I'd never met either of them, and they arrived a little early for their appointment. I was in my office concluding another counseling session when I heard a loud voice coming from down the hallway say, "We're here to see Steve Wilson."

A few minutes later I went to the lobby to greet the couple. "Hi, I'm Steve Wilson," I said. Bob walked toward me, a full ten feet in front of his wife, and said, "Hi, I'm Bob and this is Molly."

As we walked toward my office, Bob maintained a dismissive distance between himself and his wife; the tension between the two was palpable. Once we were inside my office with the door closed, I said, "So, tell me why the two of you are here."

That's when Bob unloaded on Molly: "Tell him. You tell him why we're here! You know why we're here, so why don't you go ahead and tell him. You had an affair!" Bob's badgering went on a full thirty seconds, though it seemed more like an hour to me. I finally said, "Whoa, whoa, whoa!"

Molly's head was down the whole time Bob was demanding she tell me why they were in my office. I gently asked Bob to sit down, and then I said, "Bob, let me tell you why you are here. Molly had an affair because you are a jerk!" At that moment, Molly's head popped back up, and she looked at me as if to say, "Somebody understands me."

Let me be clear: there is never *any* excuse for an affair. Yet, sadly, Debbie and I have seen this situation play out again and again over the years. The words and actions coming from one spouse leave the other spouse feeling so devalued that he or she becomes vulnerable to the attention of another.

Nobody wakes up one morning and decides to have an affair. However, complimentary words such as "You did a great job," "You look nice today," or "You're really good at what you do," when coming from someone other than a spouse are a powerful enticement to a hurting heart that desires to feel valued. The Bible says, "But each one is tempted when he is drawn away by his own desires and enticed. Then, when desire has conceived, it gives birth to sin" (James 1:14–15).

A man or woman who is hurting may reason, "You know, my spouse hasn't said anything nice to me in what seems like forever." When the hurting spouse's desire to feel valued "has conceived," as James 1:15 says, the result is all too often an extramarital affair.

Again, I am not condoning this behavior. It doesn't matter whom we're married to; if we made the vow "for richer, for poorer; for better, for worse," we are in covenant with both our spouse and God.

There are times in every marriage when the cord that binds us to our spouse becomes frayed. However, we can always depend on God's steadfast love to hold us together. That's why the Bible says, "Again, if two lie down together, they will keep warm; but how can one be warm alone? Though one may be overpowered by another, two can withstand him. And a threefold cord is not quickly broken" (Ecclesiastes 4:11–12).

It's not unusual for us to marry someone whose personality

is the exact opposite of ours. Those who have quiet, mellow personalities usually marry someone who likes to be heard, who has a dominant personality. We've all heard the expression, opposites attract. The problem is, once opposites attract and marry, they attack. This is especially true once they hit the opinion level of communication.

Things go fine for a while in such marriages because the opinionated spouses are so busy listening to themselves, they don't really hear their quiet spouse. They think, *Well, my wife [or husband] wants me to make all of the decisions, so I'm going to make them.* Dominant spouses are often so unaware of what's going on around them, they never notice when their spouse's head begins to fall in defeat because he or she feels so devalued.

To safely navigate the whitewater rapids of opinions in a marriage, you first need to determine who's the more opinionated one. You've got to be honest with yourself—and with God. The best place to start is by praying this prayer from Psalms 139:23–24: "Search me, O God, and know my heart; try me, and know my anxieties; and see if there is any wicked way in me, and lead me in the way everlasting."

◆

Are You Stripping Value or Adding It?

In our marriage, I am the more highly opinionated one. And yet it was me who, seven years into our marriage, felt our disconnection most acutely.

I desperately wanted Steve to talk to me, but I see now that every time he talked to me, I responded with criticism. For example, as we drove home every Sunday after church, our conversation would go something like this:

"That was a great sermon today, wasn't it?" I'd ask.

"It was," Steve would reply.

I'd say, "Tell me what you got out of it."

Steve would proceed to tell me how the message affected him, and then I'd say, "Really? How did you get that?"

In essence, I was telling Steve that what I got out of the message was far superior and more holy than what he got. This went on for years without my realizing what I was doing. Steve even came up with an avoidance tactic so that he wouldn't have to feel the sting of my critical words. When I'd ask him what he got out of the sermon, he'd say, "Oh, I don't know. What did you get?"

It wasn't until we made the decision to be honest with each other that I saw what I was doing. One day Steve told me, "You know, Debbie, I think what I have to say is kind of important."

"It is," I agreed.

"No, it isn't. You think what you say is much more important," Steve said.

And he was right.

Being strongly opinionated enhances productivity in some situations, but left unchecked, it can strip value from those we love most—our spouses and children. Who wants to live in a home where family members feel like they can never win because they don't measure up?

Once I realized what I'd been doing to my family, I

had to make a conscious decision. I told myself, "I want people to feel more valued and loved when they are *with me*, not when they are apart from me." I *wanted* to value my husband, my children, and my friends, but I knew I first had to change the way I thought.

When I turned to my Bible for guidance, I saw that it said, "And do not be conformed to this world, but be transformed by the renewing of your mind, that you may prove what is that good and acceptable and perfect will of God" (Romans 12:2). I learned to be quiet and be a better listener. When I was tempted to negate what someone else said by offering my opinion, I'd tell myself, "Don't go there, Debbie. Ask a question and find out about their heart." At first my questions were short and simple: "Tell me more." "Tell me why you feel that way." I learned that whether it was Steve, one of our children, or a friend I talked to in this new way, the person walked away from our conversation feeling valued and loved.

God has extended His grace to us, so why shouldn't we also extend grace to those in our household—especially our spouse? What does that behavior look like? Perhaps instead of offering our own opinion or criticism, we remember what it was that we first loved about our mate and realize that quality is still there. Instead of stripping value from the one we love, we pour worth into our spouse with our words. This means we spend less time talking and more time listening. It means we ask our spouse what he or she feels and thinks, and then truly listen to the answer.

A specific conversation starter on date night might be to ask your spouse, "What do I do that shows you I value you?" When Steve first asked me this question, I couldn't help but think back to when I felt exactly the opposite. We had hit that twelve-year mark in our marriage and I felt everyone else in the church was more important to him than I was. How the man has changed since then! In answering his question, I said, "Steve, you have no idea, but whenever we go someplace together—even if we are on opposite sides of a room—when I look for you and find your eyes, they always say, 'You are the most beautiful woman in the room.'"

Another thing Steve does is that when we sit down together, he puts his arm around me. This says to me "She's mine. I'm going to love her and protect her."

Letting our spouses know the ways they make us feel valued only affirms their own value in our eyes.

———————◆———————

Steve

The Bible speaks to men about their relationships with their wives, saying, "Husbands, love your wives, just as Christ also loved the church and gave Himself for her. So husbands ought to love their own wives as their own bodies; he who loves his wife loves himself" (Ephesians 5:25, 28).

Men, you have to love your wife enough to die for her. You've got to be her greatest cheerleader. You have to be the person who says, "You know what, honey, I'm in this for better or worse, for richer or poorer. I'm going to value you. I'm going to pour worth into you."

When you take the time to pour value into your wife, it will automatically pour over into your children.

If It Isn't Profitable, Get Rid of It!

In Paul's letter to Titus, he talked about setting the local church in order by avoiding dissension: "But avoid foolish disputes, genealogies, contentions, and striving ... for they are unprofitable and useless" (Titus 3:9). If we are going to set our marriages and homes in order through effective communication, then we, too, need to get rid of anything that isn't profitable.

As Debbie and I ventured into a new level of truth regarding our communication, we identified four specific "communication killers" that we needed to eliminate from every conversation. We knew that failure to do so would send us straight back to the baby pool of small talk and facts. These four communication killers are:

- Criticism
- Contempt
- Defensiveness
- Stonewalling

Criticism always attacks the person, not the problem. We need to be careful not to attack our spouse, who is not our enemy. We must learn to deal effectively with the problem and leave insults out of our conversation.

Contempt manifests in name-calling, sarcasm, eye rolling, and hostile humor—all of which convey disgust. Contempt really boils down to a "one up" mentality in those who display this behavior, all in an attempt to make themselves feel better. Sadly, this behavior only fractures a relationship, making it harder to heal. Contempt is the opposite of humility.

Defensiveness is the most-used weapon of choice when we

argue. It is a tool used to avoid conflict and place the blame on the other spouse. In essence, defensiveness says, "The problem isn't me; it's you!"

Stonewalling is a dangerous tactic we use to tune out our spouse and walk away. Stonewalling is the height of apathy. When we stonewall, we disengage from our spouse, removing ourselves emotionally from the situation. When this happens, the repair work takes twice as long.

For Debbie and me, eliminating these four communication killers from our relationship marked significant progress through the whitewater rapids of communication. We began to feel like Joshua and Caleb must have when they gave the positive report on the giants in the land God had promised them: "Let us go up at once and take possession, for we are well able to overcome" (Numbers 13:30).

In the next two chapters, Debbie and I will show you how we overcame two additional giants we faced on our journey to wholeness: *expectations* and *conflict*.

5

The Problem with Expectations

> *"You know that I had the kingdom right in my hands and everyone expected me to be king, and then the whole thing backfired and the kingdom landed in my brother's lap."*
> 1 Kings 2:15 *THE MESSAGE*

As King David approached death, he summoned his son Solomon so that he could turn over the kingdom, saying, "Keep the charge of the LORD your God ... that the LORD may fulfill His word which He spoke concerning me " (1 Kings 2:3, 4).

It was God's will that Solomon succeed his father as king. However, David had an elder son, Adonijah, who, along with all of Israel, expected to be named king. Adonijah voiced his expectations, and in the end, those expectations caused his death.

I'm certainly not implying that our expectations can kill us, yet they do have the power to backfire and cause us plenty of problems. The reason for this complication is that we often base our expectations on the desires of our soul (our mind, will, and emotions) rather than the Word of God.

The apostle Paul knew to keep his expectations grounded in Christ during times of trouble: "For I know that this will turn out for my deliverance through your prayer and the supply of the Spirit of Jesus Christ, according to my *earnest expectation* and hope that in nothing I shall be ashamed" (Philippians 1:19–20 *italics added*).

One of the things Debbie and I discovered when we began to practice being honest with honor was this: the expectations she had brought into our marriage were actually the root cause of some of our communication problems. Over time, we identified what we refer to as the three "bad boys" of expectation: *unspoken expectations, unmet expectations,* and *unrealistic expectations.*

But this is Debbie's story to tell.

Unspoken Expectations

I want you to think back to the time when you got married. If you are like most other people, you brought with you certain expectations of what your marriage was going to look like. Perhaps one of your expectations was that your mate was going to value you for the rest of your life. This is not a bad expectation. However, problems can arise when we never clearly identify our expectations.

One of my expectations about our marriage was that

Steve would be romantic. Remember now, our relationship started out with long-distance dating. The thing is, during the time we did spend together, I never saw Steve display any signs of what I thought romance looked like. Isn't it funny how we think that after we get married, things are going to be different? That's exactly what I thought. But what I learned was this: unspoken expectations will always lead to discouragement.

That's what happened to Steve and me. For instance, I had it in my head there would be times when he would call me in the afternoon and say, "Hey, honey, how are you?" and I would say, "I'm good. How are you?" He'd say, "I'm great. Listen, I have an idea. I know you probably already have supper planned, but I want you to put everything away. I've already arranged for a babysitter to come to the house, and I want you to be dressed and ready to leave at six o'clock. I'm taking you out to dinner."

I entertained this idea over and over throughout the first twelve years of our marriage, and I can tell you that the days I dwelt on it were not good days for either of us. Steve would walk in the door at five-thirty as he always did, and ask, "How are you?" I'd give him a one-word answer, *fine.* He'd ask if anything was wrong, and I'd again give a one-word answer, *nope.* Then I would punish him all night long because he hadn't taken me out for a surprise dinner. By the time we went to bed, we were both discouraged about our relationship, and poor Steve didn't have a clue why I was mad.

After Steve and I got on the backside of the twelve-year mark of our marriage, we were taking one day when he said, "Hey, can I ask you a question?" When I said yes, he continued by telling me that for quite a few years in our marriage, I had seemed angry with him. Then he said, "Can you tell me why?"

I laughed to myself and thought, *Okay, I'm finally going to tell him what I desperately wanted him to figure out through my ugly disposition.*

"Steve, I wanted you to be romantic."

"Me, too," he said with a laugh. "Now what does that look like?" We both laughed and then he said, "If you will help me, I want to be romantic." So I decided to tell him what I wanted (which I should have done years earlier). As we laughed and pondered those years, I came up with an idea.

"Steve, why don't you bring me something every Friday that simply shows you are thinking of me. That would be romantic to me. And please know that I'm not talking about expensive things, rather something that shows you are in tune with me."

Steve agreed and willingly said that was what he would do. So on the first Friday, I grew more excited with each passing hour as I anticipated what he might bring to me. About five-thirty that evening, he walked into the kitchen with his chest out and his hand behind his back and said *hey* like men do when they feel they've done something good.

I returned his *hey* and said, "What's behind your back?"

"I've got something for you."

"What is it?"

He pulled his hand from behind his back and held out a Snickers bar. Okay, I know Snickers bars are great, but it wasn't my favorite candy. It had no significance for me whatsoever. Seeing the look of pure happiness on his face, I knew I couldn't blow the moment. Besides, as a psychologist, Steve had often said during the years we were raising our children that positive behavior must always be affirmed.

So being quick on my feet, I kissed him on the cheek and thanked him. He walked out of the kitchen thinking he was "the man" as I opened a drawer and placed the Snickers bar inside, thinking, *God, this has got to get better.* Now, before I tell you what Steve brought me the next Friday you need to know he is not by any means a risk taker. So guess what I got on the second Friday? You got it—another Snickers bar! At that point I realized I needed to drop that particular expectation.

Sadly, for years I'd dwelt on what Steve *wasn't* and I'd totally forgotten who he *was*. Steve was, and is, an incredible husband who always puts my needs before his own. He has an amazing heart for his family and for the others God has entrusted to him. Most of all, he is the best "pops" our grandkids could ever ask for.

Please don't forget who your spouse was when you got married. Your mate still has the qualities that first drew you to him (or her). I couldn't see that truth even when it was right before my eyes.

Long story short, my unspoken expectations spawned years of disappointment as those expectations went unmet.

Unmet Expectations

If you are the "high expectation" spouse in your marriage, perhaps you should take a look at the reason why. I say this because we can set our expectations so high that neither our spouse nor our children can meet them. For example, I remember one day when Steve decided to make our bed, which was a good thing. But when I walked into the room and saw the haphazard manner in which he'd placed the decorative accent pillows, the first thing I said was, "If you're not going to make the bed correctly, don't make it at all." He said okay and walked away. That's when I figured out that his making the bed 80 percent correctly and my fixing the 20 percent was actually a good thing for both of us.

You may not realize it, but your spouse and family may be greatly discouraged right now because no matter what they do, it's not good enough. Let me ask this question: does anybody ever get a "win" in your home?

If we're honest, we often tend to be high on criticism and low on affirmation in our homes. If this is true in your home, have you considered the effects on your household? When we don't positively affirm our spouse and children, it leaves them vulnerable as they walk out into the world.

When Steve and I began having children, one thing he said we were going to do was build them up. I agreed with him, although at first I didn't really understand what this looked like since I hadn't grown up in an affirming environment. I loved watching Steve tell our children on a regular basis they were the greatest. He would introduce them like this: "Meet Josh; he is the greatest sixth grader. Meet Jordan; he is in the third grade. And meet Janae, the world's greatest kindergartner!" Jordan would pull on Steve's pant leg and say, "Dad! You didn't say I was the *greatest* third grader."

Our children believed what their dad said about them. Not only did it allow them to be okay as they walked through a cruel world, it also readied their hearts to believe what God said about them.

When we never take the time to affirm our spouses, they become vulnerable to the flattery of the world. A woman may receive a compliment on her hair from a man she works with, which makes her feel good. She may think to herself, *My husband doesn't even know I have hair because he never compliments me on anything.*

God has called us to be encouragers—especially for our spouse and children. You may say, "But Debbie, I can't be an encourager because I was never encouraged." That's just an excuse!

Steve and I were watching *The Biggest Loser* on television one night. In the final workout of that week's program, the trainer was pushing one man to work harder and harder on the treadmill. All the while the man was griping and complaining. The trainer finally had enough and hit the emergency stop button. This jolted the man, who said, "What? Why did you do that?"

"Nothing in your life will ever change until you run out of excuses," the trainer said.

Those are powerful words we need to take to heart when encouraging our spouse and children. We must *choose* to give each member of our family the affirmation they need, whether or not we get it back in return. God has entrusted us to be encouragers—no matter what. I had to confess to Steve that I was guilty of not being an encourager.

For years I literally fell in love with Steve over and over every Sunday because of his ability to encourage others. In all six of the churches where he served as either a youth or family minister for thirty years, the senior pastor would always offer an invitation for people to make a public decision in response to the gospel. Steve would stand at the front of the sanctuary to receive those people because he understood how frightening and intimidating it was to step out.

Once the people would begin walking down the aisle, Steve wouldn't merely stand and wait for them to come; he would start walking toward them. I would watch as my husband met them halfway and then took them in his arms and rejoiced with them, oftentimes crying with them. I'd stand at my pew with tears in my eyes and think, *God, how did you ever choose me to be married to this man?* I would be overwhelmed with love for who Steve was.

Nonetheless, by the time church was over and I'd rounded up our three kids (who would usually be arguing about what to do for lunch), I'd have lost that loving feeling.

So did I ever tell Steve how I felt? No. But the truth is, had he done something wrong that morning, I would have found a way to tell him before we ever left the building. This is the truth of who I really was, and the reason why it was so hard for anyone to live up to expectations in our home.

Would you dare to do some self-examination and ask yourself if your spouse and children ever get a "win" ... or do they always "lose"?

Unrealistic Expectations

While both men and women are capable of giving birth to unrealistic expectations, I want to take a moment to speak directly to an area of vulnerability that women often experience more intensely than men: expectations based on worldly stimuli.

The psalmist wrote, "I will walk in my house in integrity and with a blameless heart. I will set no worthless or wicked thing before my eyes" (Psalms 101:2–3 AMP). And Jesus said, "Take heed what you hear" (Mark 4:24). Can it be that what we allow our eyes to see and our ears to hear will influence our expectations? I believe the answer is *yes*.

For this reason I caution women and girls to be careful what they watch and read. Romance novels are created to elicit strong emotional responses from readers, but they are based on false images and unrealistic ideals. Never allow the world to dictate your expectations for marriage. Understand that God has a plan for your life. It's a good plan, based on the promises in His Word—not on romance novels, fairy tales, or movies.

When God began to reveal to me that my expectations for my marriage were unrealistic, He spoke to my heart and said, "Debbie, when you walked into your marriage all those years ago, you walked into your house and hung on your wall an imaginary picture of what your marriage would look like."

As always, God was right.

I thought my husband would take me out for a romantic dinner; instead, I got a Snickers bar. I thought we would have one boy and one girl; instead, we had two boys and one girl. I thought we'd live in the same house for a long time; we are now living in our seventeenth home in thirty-five years. The sad thing is, I was continually beating Steve up emotionally over my unrealistic expectations. That's when God said to me, "Debbie, it's time for you to tear up that picture and instead value your husband."

And that's exactly what I did.

Having expectations isn't necessarily a bad thing. God has made numerous promises in His Word, and when we mix our faith with them, we can confidently expect the promised result. Even so, we must always be willing to release our expectations to God, for the Bible tells us, "Many are the plans in a person's heart, but it is the LORD's purpose that prevails" (Proverbs 19:21 NIV).

6

Dealing with Conflict

> *For the weapons of our warfare are not carnal*
> *but mighty in God for pulling down strongholds,*
> *casting down arguments and every high thing*
> *that exalts itself against the knowledge of God,*
> *bringing every thought into captivity to the*
> *obedience of Christ."*
> 2 Corinthians 10:4–5

You cannot live with another human being—no matter how much you love the person—without experiencing conflict at some time or another. Conflict arises when opinions clash. No two people see eye to eye all the time. Of course, what that conflict looks like in a marriage varies according to each spouse's personality type, values, and upbringing.

For instance, Debbie grew up in a home where her parents fought on a regular basis. They never left each other, so Debbie assumed that when you were married, you fought. She didn't see fighting as a bad thing; it was just something married people did.

When we were first married, I wouldn't fight with Debbie. There were times when she'd be railing about something we disagreed on, and when she'd stop, I'd look at her and say, "Are you finished?" She'd say, "Well, no, I'm not." Then she would find some additional issue to use as an attack tool, and before long I'd be engaged in the battle, meeting her blow-by-verbal blow. The only thing either of us was interested in at that point was winning.

Have you ever been in an argument that escalated to the point that something came out of your mouth that made you think, *Uh-oh, I wish I hadn't said that*? Perhaps in an effort to one-up your spouse, you pulled out some old artillery; you brought up something he or she had done years earlier. When the argument was over, you felt pretty good because you'd won—even though your spouse had been mortally wounded by your words. That's when you said, "I'm sorry, I didn't mean any of that." But it was too late; the words couldn't be taken back.

This scenario is like squeezing toothpaste from its tube; you can't put it back. Debbie and I did this a lot, even when our children were in the house. There were times when our middle child would come and look at us with eyes that said, "Would you please quit?" Seeing his face would nearly break my heart. The troubling thing was, I never knew how many of our hurtful words he'd actually heard.

Debbie and I were desperate to learn how to communicate—and even disagree—in a healthy way. We decided we needed a code word that we could use to call "time out" whenever a disagreement began to escalate. We wanted to avoid saying things to each other that we knew we'd regret, and we wanted to come up with something that would break the tension and perhaps make us smile. Since we both liked Diet Coke, we decided to make it our code word.

But then came the hard part. Once the code word was invoked, what would we do next? After some honest deliberation we came up with these four rules:

Rule Number 1: When the code word is invoked by either spouse, the conversation is over. If one of us says, "I think I need a Diet Coke," the other one is not allowed to get the last word by saying something like "Well, I guess you do!"

Rule Number 2: We will take a cooling-off period. One of us will go to the right, the other to the left. But nobody will leave the house; nobody will be abandoned.

Rule Number 3: We will come back together and talk about the issue before we go to bed for the night.

Rule Number 4: We will come to a resolve. Dictionary.com defines *resolve* as "a resolution or determination made, as to follow some course of action; firmness of purpose or intent." Coming to a resolve is not about who wins or loses the argument; it's about coming to a mutual intent.

As Debbie and I discovered, the code word can come in handy at other times as well. For example, Debbie says I'm notorious for telling people things she doesn't want them to know (okay, I'm a work in progress). When we'd be dining with other couples and she wanted to alert me that she wasn't pleased with something I was saying, the under-the-table kick turned out to be a futile effort. Invariably, I'd ask her why she was kicking me, which would make her the center of unwanted attention.

I remember the first night Debbie used the code word in public. We were in a nice restaurant with friends waiting for our food and I was in the middle of telling what was, apparently, a forbidden story. Debbie gently put her hand on mine and said, "Steve, honey, I need a Diet Coke."

"You've got one right in front of you," I said, pointing out the obvious.

"Well, then, I think I need another one!"

Ah-ha, I thought. *She's telling me in a nice way to shut up.* And so I did.

As Debbie and I discovered firsthand, changing deep-seated behaviors takes both determination and effort. When it came to dealing with conflict, we found that using a code word was an effective tool in enabling us to deepen our communication—and thus improve our marriage. Not only that, but after sharing our experience at conferences and seminars over the years and seeing couples employ this method, we've seen significant changes in the marriages of others as well.

The only problem we have with our code word today is that everybody knows what it is. Anytime we order a Diet Coke, someone will invariably ask if we are fighting.

"No," we tell them. "We really do want a Diet Coke."

Not long ago, Steve and I were counseling a couple—let's call them Russ and Pat—who had been married about forty years. By his own admission, Russ was a real jerk.

They started meeting with us because the wheels had fallen off their marriage. Pat's dad had recently died, and she'd inherited his house and a nice sum of money. That's when she told Russ, "I'm out of here."

He never saw it coming; he had no idea his wife was unhappy.

In one of our first sessions, I said to Pat, "So tell us some of the things Russ does that you don't like; help us understand what's going on with you."

"Well, Debbie, how would you feel if Steve sat at the dinner table and shook his glass at you when it was empty instead of asking for a refill?"

I remember thinking, *Are you kidding me?* Then I asked Pat, "Did you always get up and get him something to drink?"

"I did—for forty years!"

As we delved deeper into their issues and their personalities, we found out they were both fighters. They'd fought a lot over the past four decades, and they were still fighting. So we explained the code word to them, gave them the rules, and then told them to choose their own code word before they left our office that day. That's when Pat started laughing. "All I can think of is *Eskimo,*" she said. Russ looked at her and said, "Eskimo it is, then."

The changes in Russ and Pat and their marriage didn't happen overnight. I remember after one particularly challenging counseling appointment, Russ looked at Steve with tears in his eyes and said, "I'm going to be your prize student."

And you know what, he was true to his word. Russ is not a jerk anymore. He and Pat have learned how to communicate. They're not beating each other up as they once did; instead, they're building each other up with their words.

We know Russ and Pat's grown children, and one of them told Steve, "Man, I don't know what happened to Dad, but I like it." Russ said, "I can tell you what happened. I'm talking what I believe. I'm living the way Jesus wants me to live."

Steve recently called to check on Russ and Pat. When he asked how they were doing, Russ said, "Steve, we're doing pretty good. We say 'Eskimo' a lot—but we're doing pretty good."

Steve

We've spent an extra bit of time hanging out at level three, opinions. That's because when we hit this level, many strongly opinionated people get stuck here. It's much easier for them to go back to small talk and sharing facts than to examine their own hearts. Facing the realization that their attitude and words have damaged their marriage, and often their entire family, is not an easy thing to do.

Navigating the whitewater rapids of opinions and learning to deal with conflict takes effort; it takes conviction. But the Bible makes this promise: "God is our refuge and strength, a very present help in trouble" (Psalms 46:1). We have the Holy Spirit to teach us and to help us. We *can* learn how to build value into our spouse and family. We *can* learn how to be quiet, and how to listen more.

You can't skip level three, which is the level you must master to be able to go deeper. This level takes time and lots of practice to get it right, so take your time and let the changes become a lifestyle, not a temporary change! Don't skip level three. Choose to embrace it and the health it brings to your marriage relationship as you move into the deep end of the communication pool.

7

Building Safety in Your Marriage and Home

> *Say this: "GOD, you're my refuge. I trust in you
> and I'm safe!" His huge outstretched arms protect
> you—under them you're perfectly safe.*
> Psalms 91:2, 4 *THE MESSAGE*

Have you ever wondered why unfiltered anger is the emotion we most frequently express in our homes? Not only was an anger-filled environment the kind of home I was raised in, but Debbie and I also modeled angry behavior in our own home during the early years of our marriage.

Neither of us ever stopped to ask ourselves, "How is everyone in the house going to feel when I vent my anger?" Of all the emotions we can express in our homes, why do we release the deadliest one? Why not convey love instead?

There were times when I would watch Debbie demonstrate such tenderness as she put our children to bed at night, and I'd think, *Wow, I really do love her.* But nine times out of ten, I wouldn't make the effort to tell her. I guess I was like the crusty old man who said, "I told my wife on the day we got married forty years ago that I loved her—and I'd let her know if that ever changed. Well, it ain't changed!"

Why is it that we spend less time praising our mates for their good qualities than we do criticizing their faults and letting them know what we think about every little thing they do wrong? The Bible says, "Out of the same mouth proceed blessing and cursing. My brethren, these things ought not to be so" (James 3:10). The Word also admonishes us, saying, "Put away from you a deceitful mouth, and put perverse lips far from you" (Proverbs 4:24).

Changing a habit, or pattern of behavior, isn't easy—especially if a particular behavior was the norm in our family when we were growing up. Any such change requires two choices. When it comes to building safety in our marriages and homes, we must first *choose* to put an end to any kind of corrupt communication or behavior that is harmful to our spouse and children. Second, we must *choose* to walk in love. The Bible says, "Love suffers long and is kind; love does not envy; love does not parade itself, it is not puffed up; does not behave rudely, does not seek its own, is not provoked, thinks no evil. Love never fails" (1 Corinthians 13:4–5, 8).

◆

I remember times in my childhood when I would cry and my parents would say, "You'd better stop that crying, or I'll give you something to cry about." We probably all heard something like that at one time or another but, as children, how did we process it? I realized I had to keep my emotions to myself because, obviously, no one wanted to deal with them. In my child's mind I rationalized that crying must make others feel uncomfortable.

If we are honest about how we feel as adults, our attitude when someone cries is often this: Stop crying because you are making me feel uncomfortable!

No one is comfortable with emotions that accompany hurt, pain, or disappointment. We know how to lash back at anger, but we are awkward and uncomfortable with tears.

When I was in the second grade, I went with my mom and dad to a parent-teacher conference. I remember sitting there as my teacher told my parents they would never have to worry about me. She said I was a strong, independent girl who would make something of herself.

Although my teacher's praise made me feel proud, I had no idea what the ramifications of those words would be. Today, I identify that parent-teacher conference as the point when my parents stopped nurturing me, expecting instead that I would always be strong and in control. I believe these expectations are what first caused me to feel no one cared about my emotions.

Fast forward fifty-something years, and I found myself having to live with those expectations while facing the hardest days of my life. When my dad died unexpectedly, grief was not an option for me as I helped plan his funeral. Then, at the funeral, my brother (my only sibling), who had been diagnosed two years earlier with esophageal cancer, informed us that the next step in his battle was hospice.

At that point, not only did I have to be strong for my mother, but I also had to help my sister-in-law and niece and nephew deal with this news. Steve and I spent the next four weeks driving back and forth to Houston, watching my brother's steady decline. He died one month to the day following my dad's death. But I was strong through it all—because that was what was expected of me.

I quickly learned that grief will not leave you alone. Grief and tears are God's way of healing the human heart. Four weeks after my brother passed away, grief hit me like a proverbial ton of bricks. Talk about tears; they flooded over me.

Looking back, I now think I was crying out years of tears I had never allowed to flow. In our marriage, I'd assumed Steve was uncomfortable with my tears; therefore, I'd always kept my emotions and feelings in check until I was alone.

At this level of communication, Steve and I realized it was time to allow each other to really *feel*.

Steve

In chapter 2, we talked about the big green chair Debbie and I purchased to resuscitate our marriage when we returned home from the beach. In a sense, Debbie and I were both grieving so many things at that time: the loss of the tender love we had first felt for each other more than a decade earlier, the finality of unmet expectations, and the loss of our married life as we had known it to that point. Still, I'm certain Debbie felt these things more intensely than I did.

The Bible says there is "a time to break down, and a time to build up; a time to weep, and a time to laugh; a time to mourn, and a time to dance" (Ecclesiastes 3:3–4). Sadly for many couples, when it comes time to mourn, they are unable to do it together. This is because they've never built safety into their relationship or their home.

As a man, I desperately wanted to try to fix things for my wife; she was hurting. I wanted to say the right thing, do the right thing. What I didn't realize was that what she needed from me was simply a shoulder to cry on. I couldn't even offer her that because we'd never developed that kind of emotional intimacy as a couple nor a safe environment in our home. But I can tell you, the Lord was gracious as He worked with me to develop new behaviors that built safety in our marriage and home.

I can remember saying to Debbie, "Come sit with me in the big chair."

"Where are you going to put your hands?" she'd ask.

"I promise I'll keep one hand in my lap and the other on your shoulder."

"You promise?"

"Yes."

"Okay, then, I'll come sit with you."

I know this sounds funny now, but it wasn't at the time. For many of you who are reading this book, it isn't funny either. Building safety is a serious, deepwater communication issue that many couples are not willing to deal with.

When it comes to building the kind of safety required to produce intimacy—and I'm not talking about sex—you cannot break your mate's trust. Establishing true spiritual intimacy with your spouse produces the kind of love that transcends natural feelings and emotions. It's the God-kind of love that makes you fall more in love not only with your mate, but with Jesus as well. It's a safe kind of love—the kind of love that that you can rely on to get you safely through the trauma that occurs when the wheels fall off of your marriage.

You may be thinking, *Easy for you to say—but I'm going through the worst time of my married life right now.* Believe me, I know exactly how you feel. The worst day of my life was the day Debbie said to me, "If this is marriage, I don't think I want it anymore."

But you know what? That day also marked the beginning of the best days of my life. Regardless of what you may be going through right now, Jesus wants to bring you to a place of wholeness and restoration—but you have to trust the process. He has given us His Holy Spirit to teach, guide, and comfort us. So hang with us as we move into level four of the deepening waters of communication, and expect Jesus to do some amazing things!

8

Expressing Feelings

> *Jesus wept. Then the Jews said, "See how He loved him!" And some of them said, "Could not this Man, who opened the eyes of the blind, also have kept this man from dying?"*
> John 11:35–37

Jesus knew before He reached the tomb of his friend Lazarus, who had been dead four days, that He was going to raise him from the dead. Yet the Bible says He openly wept.

Although Jesus was fully God, He was also fully man. Therefore, He was subject to the same emotions, or feelings, that all humans experience in response to natural situations. Throughout the gospels we see examples of Jesus expressing a variety of emotions including joy, sadness, and even anger. Simply put, God designed us to express our feelings. But what happens when, during childhood, we are either prevented from or taught not to express our emotions? What effect does this suppression of feelings have on our relationships in adulthood?

When Debbie and I had our first child, our son Josh, we had

no clue about godly parenting. We raised Josh by the book of "trial and error." When he reached the age known as the terrible twos, we knew it was time to begin disciplining him, which we did in an age-appropriate manner. As he grew older, we invested in a wooden spoon that we applied to his behind when action was required.

Of course, Josh's response was always tears. And I'm not proud to tell you how Debbie and I handled his show of emotion. We'd say something like, "Now you go to your room. When you put your happy face back on, then you can come out." So do you know what Josh learned to do? He learned to go to his room, quickly wipe away the tears that were streaming down his face, and return to wherever Debbie and I were with a happy face.

Debbie and I always thought he was so cute when he did that. What we didn't realize was, by insisting he stop crying and get happy, we were actually crippling our son's emotions. Many of our friends who were our age at the time could remember growing up in homes where they too were trained to stifle their emotions. It was not uncommon to hear a crying child's mom or dad say, "If you don't stop that crying, I'll give you something to really cry about!"

It's no wonder that, as adults, we have no idea how to express our feelings in ways that yield positive results. Inability to express ourselves in love is the reason why so many couples "live on opposite sides of the house," so to speak. Not only do they not know *how* to deal with their emotions, their homes also are not safe places for expressing any emotion other than anger. It's much safer for them to shut down their emotions than to venture into the deep and often-frightening waters of adult communication.

Debbie and I spent a lot of time in that cushy, green chair, learning how to express our feelings to each other in a way that made both of us feel safe and valued. It took some time to get to that place of safety, but the freedom and intimacy we experienced afterward was worth the pain and effort it took to get there.

Little did we know God was preparing us to one day help others who were struggling with their relationships—including members of our own family.

Debbie

I'm going to fast-forward two decades. Josh is now a grown man, married to our precious daughter-in-law Leigh.

I'd made it clear when they married that I couldn't wait to be a grandmother. And they had made it clear to me they wanted to wait a few years before having a baby. One Sunday, about four years after they'd married, my cell phone rang as Steve and I were driving home from church. Seeing it was Josh, I answered, "Hey babe! What's up?"

"Where are you?"

"We're about fifteen minutes from home," I said. "What's going on?"

"Well then, when you get home Leigh and I will call you," he said, and then he hung up.

Steve asked me who was on the phone. When I told him it was Josh, and that he and Leigh were going to call us when we got home, Steve said, "You're going to be a grandmother."

"No, I'm not. Don't tell me that," I said.

"Yeah, you are. You're going to be a grandmother."

I said, "Steve, please don't go there. I don't want to be disappointed if that's not what they want to tell us."

A few minutes after we got home the phone rang. When I answered, Josh asked, "Mom, where's Dad?"

"He's right here," I said.

"Well, put us on speaker phone," he said. So I did.

That's when he said what we'd waited years to hear: "Are you all ready to be DeeDee and Pops?" We'd had those names ready for ourselves for years, and now we are about to become grandparents. That was one of the happiest days of my life. That night, I gave thanks to God for our family and the precious new baby that I couldn't wait to welcome.

Steve and I lived in Shreveport at the time. Josh and Leigh lived in St. Louis, so we stayed connected by phone as the pregnancy progressed. One Saturday while Steve and I were running errands together, my cell phone rang. When I saw it was Josh, I answered, "How's the daddy of my grandbaby?"

At first I thought the call had been dropped, but after a few moments Josh said, "Momma, we lost the baby." I can't even begin to articulate how I felt. I didn't know what to say, what to do. Finally, Josh said, "Momma, call my brother and sister and let them know. But tell them not to call; Leigh and I can't talk right now."

"Okay," I said. "I love you."

"I love you too," Josh said. Then he hung up.

When I turned to speak to Steve, I could see that he

already knew what had happened. I didn't have to explain it to him. He simply asked, "Do you want to go home?" Instead of saying yes, do you know what I did? I did what I'd been trained to do from childhood: I pushed my feelings down deep inside of myself, put on my happy face, and said, "No, I'm fine."

I'd been raised to believe the way you deal with trauma is to hurry up and get over it. Put on a happy face and move on. Sadly, that's how Steve and I had raised our children. That's why none of us were prepared to deal with this untimely loss. But about ten minutes later, when I was ready to face the truth and express my feelings, I said, "Steve, I am *not* okay. Please take me home."

As Steve turned the car around to head back to the house, I said, "If you don't mind, I'd really like to pack our bags and take the earliest flight available to St. Louis so that we can be with them. I don't know what else we can do."

Ever so gently, Steve said, "Debbie, we can't do that. Josh and Leigh have to walk through this by themselves right now."

So Steve and I went home and spent much of the next three days embedded in our big chair, holding each other and grieving the loss of a baby we already loved dearly but would never in this life get to know.

And then Josh called.

"How are you?" I asked.

"We're horrible. Mom, what was I supposed to feel about that baby?"

All I could think at that moment was, *This is my little boy, again walking out of his room after wiping away his tears, wearing a happy face. Exactly like we trained him to do.*

"Mom, I don't know what to do. Leigh is on one side of our house, and I'm on the other. Help me, Mom. Please help me."

I knew at that moment we had to help them learn to handle each other's hearts, just like we had learned.

"Josh, God will heal your hearts, but you're both going to have to grieve. God never intended for us to grieve alone, so here's what you need to do: When you and Leigh get home from your jobs at the end of the day today, take her in your arms and then cry together and grieve the loss of your baby. Do it again tomorrow, and the next day, for as long as it takes God to heal your hearts."

"Thanks, Mom," he said. "That's precisely what we'll do."

———————◆———————

Steve

While God was healing Josh and Leigh's hearts, Debbie and I continued to pray for them. God did indeed heal their hearts. Then, about one year after the miscarriage, Leigh gave birth to a beautiful baby girl.

Later that year, Debbie was teaching a ladies' Bible study on the book of James. She decided to ask our whole family to help her with this study. She called our kids and asked them (and me) simply to read ten verses each week and then blog what those verses meant to us. The first week we delved into James 1:2–4, "My brethren, count it all joy when you fall into various trials, knowing that the testing of your faith produces patience. But let patience have its perfect work, that you may be perfect and complete, lacking nothing." Josh participated in that study, and I want to share with you what he wrote:

"When it comes to trials, the miscarriage was the most obvious. Leigh and I have loved each other for a very long time. But never more than we do today. Losing that baby made us cling to each other and made us run to Jesus. You see, we couldn't control the situation. We just had to have faith that God would use something that devastating to do what would be best for us. And, man—He did! We learned of sin in our lives that we didn't even know was there. And we learned how to communicate better with each other. More than anything else, it allowed us to be blown away by a baby girl named Morgan Lily."

The Bible says, "Weeping may endure for a night, but joy comes in the morning" (Psalms 30:5). Talk about joy! Joy is realizing God loves us enough to allow us to go through hard times so that we can run to Him. One thing I've learned is this: we may not always understand *why* we are going through a hard time, but we can be certain God is always working things out for our ultimate good.

For Debbie and me, one of the best things we learned as an outcome of our own hard times was how to hold each other's hearts.

9

Can I Trust You to Hold My Heart?

> *The LORD is my strength and my shield; my heart trusts in Him, and I am helped; therefore my heart exults.*
> Psalms 28:7

To trust simply means to rely upon or place confidence in someone. *Trust* can be defined as the belief that someone or something is reliable, good, and honest.

The Bible tells us over and over again that we can trust God with our hearts, yet many people find this a difficult thing to do. If trusting God with our hearts is difficult, how much more so is trusting our spouse?

We've all heard the saying, "Trust is not easily given; it must be earned." Debbie and I learned that the beautiful thing about moving to the deep end of the communication pool with our spouse is this: once we've left the shallow water, navigated the whitewater rapids, established safety in our home, and learned to express our feelings with each other, we come to a place of great reward—the place where we can safely hold each other's hearts.

During the first twelve years of our marriage, I desired so many things, yet I could not vocalize those desires. But years and experience bring clarity, which is why I can now look back and understand that what I wanted more than anything from my husband was to be fully known—and still loved.

I wanted Steve to know the things I'd been through that still scared me. I wanted him to know what I needed, what my heart longed for. In light of the good, the bad, and the ugly parts of my life, I wanted him to love me. This is what I wanted then, and it is what I want still.

Sadly, when many married couples crawl into bed at night—after the lights are out and the TV is silent—the tears start pouring. I'm not necessarily talking about physical tears. I'm talking about the heart's cry deep within to have someone it can trust.

It is human nature to want someone who will care about our heart. I can clearly recall the day when I knew for certain that Steve and I were in the place of trust where we could hold each other's hearts. It happened one evening when Steve took me out for our traditional post-Christmas dinner of Mexican food. That holiday season had been particularly hectic and exciting. Our daughter, Janae, had become engaged in October, we'd had a wonderful Thanksgiving, and had finally made it through Christmas. It had been a crazy three months—in a good way.

When Steve said, "Come on, it's time for the two of us to go get some Mexican food," I said, "Great idea—let's go!" I was frazzled, but we got in the car and went to our favorite restaurant. The hostess seated us and handed us the menus, which were really big. Once I held that menu in front of my face, all of a sudden the tears began to pour. I guess it was really the first time in weeks that I'd had time to feel.

Of course, Steve was looking at his own menu and didn't have a clue what was going on with me when he asked, "What are you going to have?" Instead of answering, I slowly lowered my menu to reveal my tears.

And you know what? He didn't respond by saying, "Whoa now, I don't know what's the matter, but can you stop? Debbie, we're in a public place." Instead, he put down his menu, reached across the table to take my hand, and asked, "What's going on?"

"Janae is getting married. I'm losing my baby," I said.

"But we're happy for her, right?"

"Yes, but I haven't been able to feel," I said. That's when the server appeared to take our order, but when he saw what was going on, he said, "I'll be back."

That was the moment I realized what I already knew: I could trust Steve to hold my heart. There is nobody else I want to be with but him. Not only does he choose to hold my heart gently, carefully, with tenderness and compassion, but he also *knows* my heart.

We had to work together to get to the place where we could safely hold each other's hearts, but it was well worth the effort.

------------- ◆ -------------

Steve

Right now, we are treading in about ten feet of communication pool water. It's not a place that many couples care to venture, primarily because they've not yet established safety in their relationships and homes.

Can you imagine how devastating it would have been if Debbie had handed me her heart, as she did at the restaurant, and I had callously bruised it by belittling her feelings or rebuking her for crying in public? Worse yet, what if she had trusted me with her heart, and then during an argument at a later time, I had used that trust she'd placed in me against her?

As we said earlier in this chapter, trust is not easily given; it must be earned. This is particularly true with couples who have had previous marriages. If a man or woman's heart has been crushed in a former relationship, it's going to be more difficult for that person to trust again.

That's why Debbie and I have written this book, why we have been so candid in sharing our own life stories, our mistakes and failures, and our triumphs and joy. I cannot help but think of Debbie—and thank God for her—each time I read this Bible verse: "The heart of her husband trusts in her [with secure confidence], and he will have no lack of gain" (Proverbs 31:11 AMP).

Believe me, what God did for us, He will certainly do for you too—if you are willing to let Him guide you to the place of trust where you and your spouse can safely hold each other's hearts.

10

Steve's Story

> *Search me, O God, and know my heart; try me and know my anxieties; and see if there is any wicked way in me, and lead me in the way everlasting.*
> Psalms 139:23–24

Before I could come to the place where I could trust Debbie with my heart, I first had to have possession of it. I was a pastor; I spent time counseling others in matters of the heart. Yet it wasn't until a tragedy took me from Shreveport to Albuquerque one weekend that I realized I wasn't in possession of my own heart.

Our second son, Jordan, was working at the Kanakuk Christian Summer Camp in Southwest Colorado, just north of Albuquerque, where we had once lived when I was on staff at a local church. One Friday, he called and said, "Hey, Dad, did you hear about Bob?" Bob was a friend of ours we had attended church with, who lived across the river from Kanakuk Camp.

"I haven't heard a thing. What's up?"

"I'm sorry, Dad, but Bob was killed in a car wreck last night. The funeral will be Monday, and I think you need to come."

I'd been working really hard, so Debbie and I agreed that I would fly to Albuquerque for the funeral and then drive to Durango, Colorado, where Jordan was, and enjoy some much-needed time off with him.

When I got to Albuquerque, I spent the night with my friend Mike. Years before, when I'd been on staff at the church in Albuquerque, Mike had been part of a group of men I spent a lot of time with. We'd all been the kind of friends who spoke truth into each other's lives.

Reunited with Mike there in Albuquerque, I shared with him about my job's responsibilities and my frustration with the heavy load of counseling that seemed never ending. I'm sure he sensed my feelings of bitterness and anger that I kept under tight control, but he didn't pry.

As I was getting ready to drive to Colorado following the funeral, Mike said, "Hey, I've got a book you need to read." He handed me a copy of *Wild at Heart* by John Eldredge.

"Well, that's great. Thanks for the book," I said.

"No, Steve, you really need to read this book."

Seeing the resolve in his eyes, I said, "Okay, I'll do it."

When I took a closer look at the book that first night in Durango, I was intrigued by the subtitle: *Discovering the Secret of a Man's Soul.* I turned to the table of contents and was reading the chapter titles when suddenly one seemed to jump off the page at me—"A Battle to Fight: The Enemy."

That title described exactly where I was spiritually. I was fighting a battle with Satan, and all of the anger and bitterness I'd struggled so hard to keep in check was consuming me. I remember thinking, *Maybe Mike is right. I do need to read this book.*

While I was getting pummeled in a battle with deadly

emotions, Colorado was experiencing a dry summer marked by scores of wildfires that scorched acres and acres of land. One fire came dangerously close to Camp Kanakuk before moving to the other side of the mountain and burning up everything in its path.

During the day as I watched firefighters battle the flames, fires seemed to be everywhere, filling every canyon and climbing every height. Likewise, during the evening as I read the book, the fire of the Holy Spirit seemed to be everywhere inside me, filling every crevice of my soul and reaching into every deep, hidden place of my heart.

I called Debbie and said, "Hey, I want to tell you about this book I'm reading and also about the fires out here. They are everywhere, and it's just crazy."

She said, "Tell me about the book."

"It's *Wild at Heart* by John Eldredge, and it's awesome."

"Well, maybe I need to go buy it," she said. And that's what she did the very next day. When I talked to her the following evening, she said, "I'm reading the book, and wow, Steve, this is you!"

"Yeah, it is, but let me tell you about the fires ..."

The next night she said, "Tell me about the book."

"It's good. Today the fire burned up a house, and it exploded!"

That's pretty much how our phone conversations went for a week while I was trying to figure out the condition of my heart. When Debbie picked me up at the airport, I could tell she was angry the minute I got in the car.

"Hey," I said.

"Hey," she responded.

"What's wrong with you?"

"Steve, I don't want to hear about the fires. Tell me about

your heart."

I couldn't put it off any longer. The game of cat and mouse was over; I had to answer Debbie's question.

"I don't have a clue where my heart is," I told her.

Has Anybody Seen My Heart?

Attending my friend Bob's funeral had a greater impact on me than I first understood. As I recalled the words of love and affirmation spoken about him and his life of service to others, I had to ask myself what people might say about me at my funeral.

I didn't like the answer.

Simply put, I had become an angry and bitter person. Worse yet, I was so consumed with my work and my concern over finances that I wasn't truly engaged with my own children—although I loved them dearly. Anytime one of them suggested we do something as a family, my standard answer was, "No, we can't."

Without realizing it, I had also shut Debbie out of my hurting heart.

That July I started on a six-month journey in search of my heart. I didn't want to be the angry husband and father who only said no, no, *no* to those I loved the most. I needed God's help and Debbie's love—and I got both. I allowed God to truly search my heart and reveal the iniquity that had crept into it, and I chose to open my heart fully to Debbie. That's when I began to feel again—and it was good.

At Christmastime that year, the kids all came home as usual. We opened presents in the morning, and then had dinner around two o'clock, as is our custom. As we sat around the table following our meal, I said, "Okay, everyone, tell us what you're thankful for."

Josh said, "Hey, Dad, it's good to have you back."

"It's good to have me back? What do you mean?" I asked.

"I don't know, Dad, but for the last few years everything that came out of your mouth began with the word no," he said.

"So how do you know I'm back?" I asked.

"Remember the other day when you were lying in front of the fireplace and I jumped on you and bit your earlobe like you used to do to us when we were kids?"

"Yeah," I said.

"Well, you didn't get mad."

"That's because I couldn't breathe, you big 220-pound lug," I told him.

"No, Dad, if I'd done that a year ago, you would have gotten mad."

A few moments later Debbie leaned over to me and whispered, "Are you crying?" Of course, I said *no*, but the truth was, my tears that day only confirmed I was again in possession my long-lost heart.

Invest in What Matters Most

That six-month journey to finding my missing heart taught me this simple but powerful truth: I needed to invest my life in the people who would cry at my funeral.

Many men (and women too) are like I was at the time: they're giving their lives to their company or job. At the same time, their children are growing up, and I can tell you, in a blink of the eye, those kids will be grown and gone.

Think about this: Your time with your children is not replaceable. However, you *are* replaceable where you work. You can show up one morning to find out the company is downsizing and you're done.

When I resigned my position at the church where I'd been on staff, I gave them two weeks' notice, and in turn, they gave me their thanks for my years of service. Mind you, I'd given them my life during my kids' growing-up years; I'd been fully invested and involved.

On my final Friday at work, Debbie was helping me pack my books and personal items when a man appeared outside the door of my office. I'd never seen him before, so I decided to take the first step and introduce myself.

"Hey, my name is Steve," I said as I extended my hand.

"Hi, Steve, my name is John."

"Nice to meet you, John. So, what are you doing here today?" I asked.

"I'm replacing you," he said.

I wasn't even gone, yet I'd already been replaced. Never had the words of Solomon in Ecclesiastes 2:11 rung so true: "Then I looked on all the works that my hands had done and on the labor in which I had toiled; and indeed all was vanity and grasping for the wind."

I'm not saying the work I'd done at the church was meaningless. What I *am* saying is, apart from God's wisdom and love, the work we do can often lead to a life of despair—as it did for me for a period of time. I was lost in the callousness of my heart until Jesus stepped in and said, "Come on, dude, what's going on with you? [That's how He talks to me.] I want a heartbeat back in your heart so that you can love and laugh."

I realized that, regardless of where I worked, I would always be replaceable; but when it came to my family, I would never be replaceable. So I made the decision to engage fully with my family, because they matter most in my life.

It feels kind of weird now each time I bite my grown kids' earlobes, but won't that be a great memory for them to share at my funeral?

11

Debbie's Story

> *Be kindly affectionate to one another ... giving*
> *preference to one another ... rejoicing in hope, patient*
> *in tribulation, continuing steadfastly in prayer.*
> Romans 12:10

In chapter 8, Steve and I described how we continued in our home the emotionally crippling behavior we'd learned from our parents during childhood. As we've said several times, changing a pattern of behavior doesn't happen overnight; it's a process.

So it was with me as I learned how to let not only myself but also my family express our feelings in the safety of our home. I recall one specific incident that God used to teach me a valuable truth: life *isn't* all about me.

One morning as I was walking to my Sunday school class at church, I passed a friend who was walking the opposite direction. I spoke to her, but she didn't answer me. Afterward, I didn't hear a thing the teacher said in class; all I could think was, *Why didn't she talk to me?* During the main service I was so distraught over my friend's lack of a response that I couldn't worship, let alone focus on the pastor's message.

When Steve and I got into the car to go home, he looked at me and said, "What's on your mind?"

"Steve, I passed my friend Susie in the hallway this morning, and she didn't speak to me. I've been wracking my brain, trying to figure out what I may have done to hurt her feelings to the point that she won't even talk to me."

Steve is a contemplator, so it took him a few moments to respond. "I'm going to tell you a couple of things. You're not going to like the first thing I say, but I want you to hear me."

I thought, *Great. All I need is to be wounded more than I already am.* But I answered, "Okay, what?"

"First of all," he said, "you're not that important."

That's not very nice, I thought. "Okay, what's the second statement?"

"She might have had diarrhea."

"What?"

"Debbie, maybe she wasn't talking to *anybody* because she was trying to get to the bathroom."

The more I thought about it, the more I realized he was right. I shouldn't jump to some conclusion and allow my perception of a friend's behavior drive a wedge between us. As it turned out, when I saw her at church that evening, everything was fine (I guess she'd made it to the bathroom).

Look Past the Behavior to the Pain

That minor situation with my friend Susie had a major impact on my life. In addition to awakening me to the fact that life was *not* all about me, the Lord began to teach me how important it is to look past a person's behavior to see the pain. Oftentimes, we want to address someone's outward behavior when, in fact, God wants us to care enough to go deeper and uncover the pain causing the behavior. At times God also wants to use us to bring healing to a hurting heart.

When our daughter, Janae, was in high school, she was the head cheerleader of a sixteen-girl squad. When she came home one afternoon following cheerleading practice, she slammed the front door so hard that it shook the glass cabinets in the kitchen where I was busy preparing dinner. My first thought was, *Excuse me? We do not slam doors in our house.* That's exactly what I proceeded to go tell her when the Lord gently tapped me on the shoulder and said, "Debbie, what am I teaching you about looking past a person's behavior to their pain?" *Oh, yeah, right,* I thought.

Janae then went into her bedroom and slammed the door. That was the second slammed door in less than two minutes. Something was up. I had a choice: I could go in there and reprimand her for slamming the door, or I could look past her behavior and try to get her to tell me what was going on.

When I went into her room, she was standing in her bathroom with tears streaming down her face. I sat down on her bed and said, "Janae, come and sit down by me." When she did, I asked, "What's wrong?"

"Mom, I'm so tired of being head cheerleader."

"What happened?"

"My cheerleading coach told me I had to get on to the girls about their bad behavior at the football game. When I did what she asked me to do, the girls got mad at me. Now they're all planning to go do something together this weekend, and they didn't invite me. I'm done!"

We sat together quietly for a few minutes while I loved on

her, and then I said, "You know what, Janae? Leadership is a hard place for anyone. But God has called you to be a leader. I'm sorry for the way they treated you." I went on to encourage her by affirming her and telling how awesome she was at what she did. By the time we finished talking, she was doing well.

On the other hand, I *wasn't* doing too well. When I returned to the kitchen, I started crying. Not because of what had happened to my daughter, but because I realized how close I had come to adding another layer of pain to her already hurting heart.

If the Lord hadn't reminded me about looking past a person's behavior, I would've walked into her room and said, "Young lady, you come here!" I would have taken her to the front door and made her open and close it correctly. Then I would have done it again with her bedroom door. And do you know what Janae would have done? She'd have gone into her bedroom alone, thinking nobody cared about her pain.

Steve and I see this behavior played out in so many family situations, but perhaps never more acutely than in blended families, where we hear stories like this:

The wife has had a terrible day dealing with her ex, who has once again failed to send the child support payment. Her husband comes home to find her crying in the bedroom. Instead of saying, "Okay, honey, tell me what's going on," and then listening to her heart, he says, "What's wrong with you?" She says, "Nothing," so he takes her at her word and goes about his normal activities, leaving her to feel as though nobody cares.

Or a couple is dealing with one spouse's sixteen-year-old, who is behaving badly because he's still mad that his parents got a divorce and now Mom is married to somebody else who doesn't connect with him. He too feels that nobody cares.

Looking past a person's behavior—especially when it affects

everyone in the home—is not an easy choice. But it's the right choice. Jesus already knows about the pain that is at the root of a loved one's bad behavior. He's waiting for us to look past the behavior and say, "Honey, I'm here for you. Now tell me what's going on."

When we choose to hold each other's hearts, it gives us confidence that God holds our heart. "Let us therefore come boldly to the throne of grace, that we may obtain mercy and find grace to help in time of need" (Hebrews 4:16).

So what are you waiting for?

12

Understanding Needs

> *For You formed my inward parts ... I will praise You, for I am fearfully and wonderfully made; marvelous are Your works, and that my soul knows very well.*
> Psalms 139:13–14

Most of us learned in the seventh grade that the five basic human needs are oxygen, water, food, shelter, and sleep. So, you may wonder, what does understanding needs have to do with communication? Obviously, we are not talking about physical needs.

We humans are actually three-part beings comprised of spirit, soul, and body. Our spirit, made in the image of God, is the eternal part of our being; our soul consists of our mind, will, and emotions; and our body is the temporary earth suit we inhabit in this physical life.

When it comes to understanding needs as they relate to communication, we're going to focus on the soul realm of our being—in particular, our emotions.

Debbie and I have placed understanding needs at the fifth level of communication with good reason. Most people don't even know what their emotional needs are, much less being able to talk about them. This is why it's critical that we first establish a sense of safety within our marriage relationship and home so that we can effectively *communicate* with our spouse (and family members).

———————◆———————

Debbie

I'll never forget what Steve said to me the night I told him that if this was marriage, I didn't think I wanted it anymore. He said, "Whoa, whoa, whoa! Tell me what you need."

The sad thing was, I was so emotionally numb at that point that I didn't even know what I needed. I hope you never get to that crisis point, as Steve and I did. But if it happens, I can assure you, you're not going to be able to identify what you really need.

Looking back, I do remember what crossed my mind at the moment. My initial thought was, *You know what? I need you to remember to take out the garbage on Tuesday. Why is it that you can't remember every Tuesday is garbage day and you need to take it out without my having to tell you?*

I know how stupid that thinking sounds in light of what was truly important. There we were, facing the biggest crisis of our marriage, and all I wanted to do was nitpick.

As Steve and I began to dissect our relationship and then move to deeper levels of communication, God revealed the importance of discovering and understanding each other's primary need. (Of course, we know that the greatest individual need each of us has is for God. He created us with a hole, a place in our inner heart, that only He can fill.) What Steve and I discovered as we became more comfortable in sharing our feelings with each other was that we each had a primary need stemming from something that had happened to us before marriage. In both our cases, that need was only revealed after we were able to identify and express our greatest fear.

This one point is so important that I want to say it again. *If we want to know our spouses' greatest need, our relationships have to be safe enough for them to share their greatest fear.*

In chapter 6, we talked about dealing with conflict and how coming up with a code word was a great way to take a time out from arguing and diffuse a volatile situation. When Steve and I used to disagree, I was the one who was always ready for a fight. Steve, on the other hand, would not engage in a fight. I could never understand that. In fact, the more he refused to fight with me, the more I was convinced he didn't love me. I thought, *If you're not going to get in here and argue with me, then you must not care about me.* I held to this false belief for years.

As Steve and I began to dig into our lives, sharing the hurts and trauma we'd each experienced in our youth, the pieces started to come together. Steve spoke openly about his parents' tumultuous relationship and the fighting that had gone on almost daily. He recalled many times when the fighting would become so intense that his mother would grab her car keys, run out the front door, and leave. This happened over and over again while Steve was a little boy.

Then when he was in the eighth grade, his parents got into a fight on Christmas Day over a toy that hadn't been put together correctly. At eight o'clock that morning, Steve's mother left the house and didn't return until ten o'clock that night. Steve remembers, "We didn't finish opening presents until she came back. That's when I first understood that when two people fight, someone always leaves."

Once he told me this, I realized that his refusal to fight with me during the early years of our marriage had nothing to do with how much he loved me. He didn't want to fight with me because he didn't want me to leave.

In a word, my husband's greatest fear was *abandonment*. What grieves me most today is the way I opened up his biggest wound the day I said to him, "If this is marriage, I don't think I want it anymore." I hadn't known his heart well enough to understand he was afraid that I too would leave him.

But now, because I know his heart, I can meet his need for assurance that I'm not going to leave him. I talk about our future, what we're going to do, and where we're going to go. For instance, here's how I shared with him a dream of mine for our future: "Steve, when we get settled in our new home in Denton, I want a bedroom big enough for bunk beds for our grandbabies." Because he has trusted me with his heart, I want to do everything I can to instill the truth that—no matter what—I'm with him for life.

One of the nicest byproducts of our coming to understand this need is a tee shirt that we sell at our live seminars. It says, IF YOU LEAVE ME—I'M GOING WITH YOU!

◆

Steve

Getting to the place where Debbie and I could be transparent and honest with each other regarding our fears wasn't easy. The "understanding feelings" level of communication can be a scary place, but if you've already built safety into your relationship, it's also a place of freedom. What man wants to tell *anyone* that he fears abandonment? But we all have fears.

Debbie shared with me how, when she and her brother were children, their father had certain expectations of them they sometimes could not meet. Because she was a child, the only way she could process her perceived "failures" was to think, *If I don't meet my parents' expectations, they won't love me.* Because she didn't want to fail, she became a perfectionist. She came into our marriage with an "I can't fail" mentality, and guess what that made her? A control freak.

Would you believe it took twenty years of my verbal affirmations to convince Debbie my love for her was unconditional? And, believe me, she is not naturally a slow learner. I remember the day when she finally realized I didn't see her through the eyes of perfection. We were working in our flowerbeds one gorgeous spring morning and Debbie was covered with dirt from top to bottom. I looked at her and said, "You are one sexy chick! You are an awesome mom and one amazing woman. I love you."

"Are you kidding me?" she asked.

"Nope. I've been telling you for twenty years how awesome you are and how much I love you."

"You really believe that, don't you?"

"Duh," I said.

You may say, "Well, Steve, I told my wife I loved her every day for a whole week and nothing changed." Then tell her for a month, a year, or twenty years.

We have to be willing to do whatever it takes to get past our spouse's pain from the past, whether it's some kind of abuse, the pain of divorce, the death of a child, never measuring up at home, or never measuring up professionally.

As a man, I'm to be a version of "Jesus with skin" to my wife. The Bible says, "Therefore, if anyone is in Christ, he is a new creation; old things have passed away; behold, all things have become new. Now all things are of God, who has reconciled us to Himself through Jesus Christ, and has given us the ministry of reconciliation" (2 Corinthians 5:17–18). Because, along with all believers, I've been given the ministry of reconciliation, my goal is to understand Debbie's greatest fears in life so that I will know exactly what she needs.

When you and your spouse take the time to build safety into your relationship so that you can talk honestly about your fears, you'll enter a level of communication that brings with it the kind of freedom Jesus referred to when He said, "He has sent Me to heal the brokenhearted, to proclaim liberty to the captives ... to set at liberty those who are oppressed" (Luke 4:18).

13

Fear—the Enemy of the Soul

> *For God did not give us a spirit of timidity or cowardice or fear, but [He has given us a spirit] of power and of love and of sound judgment and personal discipline [abilities that result in a calm, well-balanced mind and self-control].*
> 2 Timothy 1:7 AMP

The Bible makes it clear that fear is not part of God's plan for our lives. Nevertheless, God knew that we humans would have "ample opportunity" to fear throughout our days on earth, which is why He said 365 times in the Bible, "Do not fear."

All kinds of fear exist in the world: fear of rejection, fear of abandonment, fear of death, fear of ridicule, fear of failure, fear of success—and the list could go on. Most of us are so consumed with dealing with our own fears that we don't take time to examine our spouse's life to learn what kind of fear he or she may be confronting on a daily basis—fears that were likely a part of our mate's life long before marriage.

Once we become safe enough with our spouse's heart, he

or she can begin to express the wounds brought into the marriage. As Debbie and I chose to walk into each other's lives, I remember when she became overly protective with me. As I shared some of my wounds, she vowed she would protect me from ever being hurt like that again. That was the point we realized that one of the privileges in marriage is getting the opportunity to heal hurts in our mate that we never caused. I like to tell people that God uses Debbie as the cortisone cream that heals my hurts.

I know God loves me. The Bible says, "The LORD is the light of my salvation; whom shall I fear? The LORD is the strength of my life; of whom shall I be afraid? (Psalms 27:1). I also know Debbie loves me. God's love expressed through Debbie is, for me, a picture of the perfect love described in 1 John 4:18: "There is no fear in love; but perfect love casts out fear." Love is God's antidote to fear.

A couple of years ago, we were teaching this principle in a live conference, and at the break, a couple who looked to be in their seventies approached us. The woman had tears pouring down her face, so Debbie reached out to her and said, "Tell me what's going on."

"You finally uncovered it," she said.

"What did we uncover?"

She said, "I've kept my husband at arm's-length distance for forty-something years, and I could never figure out why"

"Tell me why," Debbie said.

"When I was in the eighth grade, I was chosen homecoming queen at my school. I went home and told my mother the good news and that I was going to be honored at a parade at the school on Friday. But my mom said I couldn't be homecoming queen because she couldn't afford to buy me a dress."

"Okay, go on," Debbie said.

"When I told my teacher I had to resign, she was so sweet. She said, 'Honey, it's okay. I've got a dress you can wear.'"

The woman went on to tell us that when she got to the school on Friday morning, she went and put on the dress the teacher had brought. But it didn't fit; it was too big. The teacher took the girl into the bathroom and pinned the dress to take up the slack. But when she walked out in front of her classmates, they all laughed. That's when she made a vow she would never let anyone get close to her so that nobody would ever laugh at her again.

"I realized that for all of the years of our marriage, I've been fearful that if my husband really knew me, he would laugh at me. But after hearing what you said, I'm not afraid anymore. I don't want to keep him at a distance; I finally let my arm come down today."

———————◆———————

Debbie

When I married Steve, I didn't realize I was walking into our marriage with a yoke of low self-esteem and virtually no confidence in who I was or what I could do. Because I'd become a perfectionist in an effort to please my parents, I was always fearful I could never truly measure up. But God's love worked through my husband to blow those fears out of the water. Let me tell you how He did it.

When I was sixteen years old, I'd had my driver's license only about two weeks when I went for a drive one

Saturday morning. I was driving in the outside lane of a four-lane street, when the car in front of me on the inside lane made a rapid right turn in front of me. It happened so fast, there was nothing I could do to avoid hitting the car. I wasn't hurt, but I was really scared.

When the police arrived, the officer could see I was shaking as he took my information. He went back to his car, and then returned a few minutes later and said, "Don't worry, I've called your daddy and he's on the way." I remember thinking, *Hurry, Daddy. I'm scared.* All I wanted was for him to put his arms around me and tell me I was okay.

I'll never forget the relief I felt when Daddy drove up, got out of his car, and started walking toward me. But instead of putting his arms around me and then asking if I were okay, he said, "I can't believe you did this to the car!" The wound was immediate and deep—and I didn't know what to do with it. The unspoken message was clear: things were more important than people.

The first time I told Steve this story was after we hit our twelve-year mark and were working on our marriage. We were sitting on the bathroom floor, opening our hearts to each other, and for the first time I felt safe enough to tell him of this fear. I didn't understand it then, but God's plan for my healing had just been set in motion.

It wasn't a year later that I drove a friend of mine to a local car dealership to pick up her car, which was being serviced. It wasn't quite ready, so we decided to go get something to eat. She got back in the front seat of my Suburban, and we told our two little girls who were in the back seat that we were going to go eat. They were thrilled, and we all chatted excitedly about where to go. I put the Suburban in reverse, eased my foot off the brake, and then—bang! I backed into a brand-new car. I made sure everyone was okay and then turned my attention to the salesmen who were headed toward my vehicle, aghast at what I'd done.

The moment I saw their faces, in my mind I was again a sixteen-year-old girl who had wrecked her daddy's car. Immediately, fear came upon me. I went inside and asked if I could use someone's phone (this was before we had cell phones), and I called Steve at the church. I was shaking when he answered the phone. "Steve, I just hit a brand new car at the dealership," I said. Then I braced myself, knowing he was about to tell me I was a complete failure.

But instead of being upset about the car, the first thing Steve said was, "Are you okay? Is Janae okay?" Those six words literally wiped away years of pain. When I told him we were okay, Steve said, "Don't worry, Debbie, it's only a car. I'll take care of it." Then he told me he loved me.

"I love you, too," I said, and then I hung up the phone. The man in the office, who had heard the entire conversation, looked at me and said, "He said he loves you?" I smiled and thought, *Yes! Somebody loves me. Steve chose to heal the hurt in me that he never caused. I'm covered with cortisone cream because Steve chose to be Jesus with skin on to my wounded heart.*

I've learned it really doesn't matter what anybody thinks about me except God and my husband. And let me tell you something: I'm the apple of their eyes!

We know Jesus has already paid the price for our

healing—spirit, soul, and body. But God wants to use us to help apply His healing balm to the wounds our spouses may have experienced years before marriage. I know I spent too many years of my marriage being ruled by my fears. As a result, I constantly viewed life as being "all about me." Now that the enemy of my soul no longer rules my emotions, life is all about God again. And when life is all about God, it's only natural to want to give Him the glory. This is a lesson our little granddaughter, Morgan Lily, learned at a very young age.

Our family was recently enjoying time together at the beach when she walked up to me, put her hands on her hips, and said, "DeeDee [that's what she calls me], do you know why I exist?

I thought, *Wow, that's a big question coming from a little bitty girl.* I pondered her question for a moment and then thought, *I've got this.* I bent down to her level and said, "Morgan Lily, you exist for DeeDee to love you forever and ever!"

She said, "No, DeeDee. I exist to glorify God!"

I smiled and thought, *Wow, what will she become if she grasps that concept this early?*

It's hard to articulate what level five, expressing needs, did for my heart. When we walk around with a wounded heart, it's hard to show Jesus to anyone. He created marriage so that when our spouse chooses to love us like Christ does, we really understand the sacrificial love of God. As Steve and I became vessels God could use in one another's lives, our wounded hearts healed and then the true love began.

14

Beliefs

> *For the word of God is living and active and full of power [making it operative, energizing, and effective] ... exposing and judging the very thoughts and intentions of the heart.*
> Hebrews 4:12 AMP

The reason we titled level six "Beliefs" is that when we choose to do the hard work of communicating on a far deeper level with one another, our beliefs come alive in us. Let me explain.

Debbie and I both accepted Christ into our hearts when we were young. Yet although we believed God and His promises, because neither of us was loved unconditionally as we grew up, we couldn't grasp God's full love for us.

At times we both thought we didn't deserve God's love or, worse, that we had to earn it. We lived our lives bound by guilt rather than enjoying the freedom God desired for us. That's why our ministry verse is "that Christ may dwell in your hearts through faith; that you, being rooted and grounded in love, may be able to comprehend with all the saints what is the width and length and depth and height—to know the love of Christ which passes knowledge; that you may be filled with all the fullness of God. Now to Him who is able to do exceedingly abundantly above all that we ask or think, according to the power that works in us" (Ephesians 3:17–20).

When Debbie and I chose to love each other as Christ loves us, we gained the ability and desire to grasp God's unbelievable love for us!

Forgiveness then became easy. Many of us hold on to unforgiveness because we think it will keep us from being hurt again. Unfortunately, that is not how it works. When we forgive, we look and act most like Christ. We know this because Colossians 3:12–15 says, "Therefore, as the elect of God, holy and beloved, put on tender mercies, kindness, humility, meekness, longsuffering; bearing with one another, and forgiving one another, if anyone has a complaint against another; even as Christ forgave you, so you also must do. But above all these things put on love, which is the bond of perfection. And let the peace of God rule in your hearts, to which also you were called in one body; and be thankful."

If we hope to live our lives in a way that brings glory and honor to God, we must seek forgiveness and grant forgiveness. Ruth Graham once said, "A good marriage is made up of two good forgivers." Debbie and I believe the best way to handle forgiving is by understanding the six steps to seeking and granting forgiveness.

The six steps to seeking forgiveness are:
1. Admit what you did was wrong and hurtful.
2. Try to understand/empathize with the pain you caused.
3. Take responsibility for your actions and make restitution.
4. Assure your spouse you will not do it again.

5. Apologize and ask for forgiveness.
6. Forgive yourself.

The six steps to grant forgiveness are:

1. Acknowledge your pain and anger.
2. Be specific about future expectations and limits.
3. Give up the right to get even, but insist on being treated better in the future.
4. Let go of the blame, resentment, and negativity toward your spouse.
5. Communicate your act of forgiveness to your spouse.
6. Work toward reconciliation.

Simply put, forgiveness is choosing to untie the knot. Do you realize what living with that knot is like? When we live all knotted up, we are bound to bitterness, defensiveness, anger, and other such deadly emotions. When we choose to let the offenses go, the knot is loosened and freedom follows.

When we choose to forgive, restoration with God occurs. When we hold unforgiveness in our hearts, we break all fellowship with Him. He cannot hear us nor use us when we choose to hold unforgiveness in our hearts. I don't know about you, but I don't ever want to break fellowship with God or be unusable to Him. The moment we forgive is the moment we truly begin to live in freedom.

You may be saying, "But, Steve, I just can't put myself out there to be hurt one more time!" I understand, but do you realize that God *continuously* forgives us? Out of gratefulness for what He does for us daily, we can extend that same grace to others.

When we forgive, not only will peace reign in our hearts but our prayer lives will also become more meaningful and powerful. The most intimate thing we will ever do as husband and wife is to pray out loud with one another. It is amazing what this one choice can do in our marriage.

Let us give you six benefits of praying together as husband and wife:

1. It draws you closer to God.
2. It softens anger.
3. It makes you think of your spouse instead of yourself.
4. It causes you to feel God's presence.
5. It yields humility.
6. It strengthens your ability to hear from God without any doubts.

When you choose to do the hard work of walking deeper in the communication pool, joy and fun are sure to follow.

Men, I know we all struggle with being the spiritual leaders in our homes. Can I help you understand how to become that on a daily, consistent basis? Go past small talk and facts, and value your wife. Listen to her and eliminate any harmful words from your vocabulary. Choose to hold her heart gently by allowing her to feel and by validating her. Be safe enough that she will share her deepest wounds and fears with you. Like I say, be the cortisone cream to her heart. As you treat her in these loving ways, she will follow you into the arms of Jesus.

Women, choose to give grace to your husband and not belittle him. Value him and thank him for all he does for you and your family. Walk with him to find his heart and be careful not to squash it; allow him to be weak. Listen well as he tells you his fears, and protect his heart. When he leads, follow well and pray every day for him to be the man God designed him to be.

Okay, having let go of the things that once held you down and no longer dependent on wading in the baby pool, you can now enjoy the deep end of the communication pool where you and your spouse have freedom to swim, splash, and play!

About the Authors

Steve and Debbie Wilson are founders of Marriage Matters Now, a ministry dedicated to making a positive impact on marriages throughout the world through its live conferences, books, and teaching materials.

Steve Wilson holds a B.A. degree in psychology from William Jewel College, and a Master's degree in marriage and family counseling from Louisiana Baptist University. He spent sixteen years as a youth pastor, and then fourteen years an associate pastor of marriage and family.

Debbie Wilson holds a B.A. degree in counseling from Baylor University and Louisiana Baptist University. She has been leading marriage conferences on a full-time basis with her husband since they founded Marriage Matters Now in 2006.

Steve and Debbie have been married for 37 years and are the parents of three adult children: Josh (and wife Leigh), Jordan (and fiancé Candace), and Janae (and husband Kenny Carroll). They are also the proud grandparents of Morgan, Emmett, Hudson, and Harper. They live in Cross Roads, Texas.

For more information or to book
Steve and Debbie for a conference, go to:

www.MarriageMattersNow.com
